Are You Ready to Mainstream?

Helping Preschoolers with Learning and Behavior Problems

Are You Ready to

Helping Preschoolers with

Charles E. Merrill Publishing Company
A Bell & Howell Company
Columbus Toronto London Sydney

Mainstream?

Learning and Behavior Problems

Samuel J. Braun, M.D.

Miriam G. Lasher

Cambridge-Somerville
Mental Health and Retardation Center

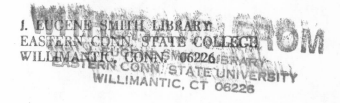

Published by Charles E. Merrill Publishing Company
A Bell & Howell Company
Columbus, Ohio 43216

This book was set in Times Roman.
The production editor was Jo Ellen Gohr.
The cover was prepared by Will Chenoweth.

International Standard Book Number: 0–675–08443–1

Library of Congress Catalog Card Number: 77–80958

1 2 3 4 5 6 7 8 9 — 83 82 81 80 79 78

Printed in the United States of America

Preface

Early childhood programs have mushroomed over the past two decades. Stimulated by research and demonstration projects, these programs suggested that intervention in the early years had a positive effect on "disadvantaged" children. Similar projects were undertaken with young special needs children. More recently, day care programs have become available to single parent families and parents who work. Because of the expansion of programs across the country, teachers have inevitably encountered more young children with special needs.

This book briefly traces some of these developments and makes some practical suggestions for programming. Our perspective is influenced by a pilot teacher training program we conducted in the Child Study Department at Tufts University for three years under the auspices of a grant from the National Institute of Mental Health (MH–10476). Those experiences were published in 1970 in *Preparing Teachers to Work with Disturbed Preschoolers,* a government-financed monograph which is now out of print. A small portion of this book appeared in that publication.

However, we derive the bulk of our experiences with very young children from our work in an interdisciplinary clinic, the Preschool Unit of the Cambridge-Somerville Mental Health and Retardation Center in Cambridge, Massachusetts. There we are involved in the assessment, treatment, and special education of young children and their families. A major portion of our time is spent consulting with staff in

Head Start, nursery schools, family day care homes, day care centers, and kindergartens located in both towns.

In preparing this book we have deliberately avoided describing our own clinical program and setting, which is psychoeducational in nature. In addition, we have not emphasized the diagnostic labeling of young children as labels too often mislead and can distract from developing a treatment plan. The young children we write about are first and foremost *children*. Their behavior often distresses adults and other children or their learning is uneven or slow. They may be "neurotic," "psychotic," "mentally retarded," "learning disabled," or "communication disordered." We hope that our approach to assessing their development, making an educational plan, and working with their parents and other community agencies can be useful for all children.

In the early chapters, we discuss ways to conceptualize classroom interventions. Assessing young children's behavior in the classroom and developing a plan to meet their special needs are highlighted. We place special emphasis on the importance of developing a close working relationship with parents. By appreciating their dilemma as parents and the crises that families confront, we believe a teacher's understanding of the human condition is greatly enhanced. In later chapters, we talk specifically about issues to consider when integrating special needs children into "normal" classrooms. Of special importance to most teachers is learning how to select and use agencies and consultants in their own communities.

This book is written for those who work directly with young children. We hope our suggestions will help you to apply what you observe while drawing from your own past experiences. We are particularly indebted to the following people who helped us learn about young children, their parents, and what a teacher can accomplish: Sylvia Woodaman Pollock, Nancy Rodman Reiser, Jane Dexter Greenspan, Dorothy M. Sang, and Sally Kear Braun. All helped to write earlier stages of some of the material that appears here. In addition, all the members of the Preschool Unit staff from 1969 to the present have been involved in this endeavor with us. We owe another kind of gratitude to Mary Ellen Delgar and Claire Murray, who typed our manuscript.

Samuel J. Braun, M.D.

Miriam G. Lasher

Cambridge, Massachusetts

Contents

Chapter One

Introduction

A special education for any child, especially a young child and his family, is truly a human process. It has to be limited in scope and in scale.

When first confronted with a young child with special needs, a teacher is likely to panic. What the child is labeled overshadows who he or she is. The thought that a teacher might be able to understand and help is far from consciousness. In fact, all that was once learned about child development or early childhood education too often seems inadequate. There is instead a frantic search for what to do, assuming that a model program exists somewhere in a book, in the head of an expert, or in some faraway city.

Perhaps the first step toward mastery is to pause long enough to get properly acquainted with the youngster. Learning to observe his behavior accurately and in a certain framework is a skill you can develop. Give yourself enough time to know what a child can and cannot do. By collecting the baseline data you will get some idea about how to help him use his strengths to confront his weaknesses. You will learn to set objectives for him and to develop approaches that are in concert with his learning style. To be truly helpful in teaching special needs children, you will have to be willing to outline tasks and carefully monitor their completion.

Such a direct approach to the teaching of young children usually raises conflicts within you about your role. Many of you have been raised on "discovery" methods of learning. Accordingly, you view yourself as a facilitator and catalyst as a child selects materials, people, and things he is interested in learning about. With most special needs children you will need to be more active—even "bossy"—and make more decisions.

Some of the decisions you make may concern using the classroom space and environment more effectively. You may have to plan for rote exercises or structured learning tasks. Other decisions may involve selecting what friends a child plays with and engineering his early efforts at relationships. You may even need to tell or show a child and his friends exactly how you want them to do things. Most teachers of young children are not accustomed to such explicit coaching or tutoring of cognitive and social skills. You may wonder if you can possibly know what is best for a young child or if you have any right to make such decisions for him. As an adult you may have to get used to answering yes. Presumably, you will assume the role of a benign dictator who remains open to changing your approach or curriculum or receiving new data. When appropriate your relationship with the child may evolve into a partnership, but probably not for some time.

As for partners, the most important ones you can have are a child's parents. You need them as colleagues. Without their help you will lack an important source of information and suggestions. You need their feedback and they need yours. The vital relationship you will need to assume with parents requires an attempt to be honest, yet tactful with a child's family: sharing your understanding and occasional feelings of frustration with tact, outlining tasks for them and setting goals much as you do for their child, and learning to respect their feelings of defensiveness as well as your own. If you can develop a close relationship you will be able to talk about those feelings. However, not all teachers or all families will wish to achieve that much mutuality or intimacy. It is, among other things, a time-consuming process.

Most teachers just beginning to work with special needs children feel a certain amount of discomfort and reluctance in working with families because they fear that their own uncertainty will be revealed. In reality, it is a most unusual family that would not resonate with the feeling of not knowing what to do. You will be surprised about how much you collectively will know and how supportive you can be to each other.

Many early childhood teachers are new to the community in which they teach or are not familiar with a network of community resources. Learning what is available is important so that you can approach a doctor, a medical facility, a nurse, a mental health clinic, or mental retardation center when it is necessary and important to do so. Most teachers hesitate, feeling they will be wasting someone's time or revealing their own ignorance, but many colleagues will be quite receptive to your questions or to the information you might share. Parents, of course, need to know that you are sharing information. More often than not, they will be relieved to have your support and will help you make contacts with resource persons.

Learning how this network of resources does or does not operate takes time, energy, and initiative. As their special needs child grows older, parents will have to rely on what is available in the community other than yourself. Although all states have passed legislation requiring that the public schools provide an education for all children with special needs, some have decided they need only serve special needs children of traditional school age. Parents may need your help to find community resources that will provide a sense of continuity to a child's treatment over time.

But your most important resource is *yourself*. By approaching the young handicapped child and his family in the way that you would want to be approached, you might discover some of the qualities that ought to exist in your program:

1. *An appreciation of the complexity of the human condition—its biological, family, and community interrelatedness*. In this sense, no one discipline corners the market and we have much to learn from one another to have a more complete understanding.
2. *A respect for the uniqueness of individual human beings, who have a variety of interests, skills, and relationships*. It is no small task to creatively synthesize a program that takes into account individual needs amongst the diversity of attitudes, feelings, and behaviors that any one person displays.
3. *A regard for your relationships with others, that they may develop into sensitive partnerships*. Your relationship with parents, in particular, is liable to be intimate as well as supportive, but not always. As a helping person you must be invested in the process of learning to listen and question.
4. *A response to others on the basis of where they are developmentally*. Above all, we should assume that all of us wish to continue to grow and need challenges.
5. *A continuing effort to make explicit those areas identified as strengths, so as to help with weaknesses*. The explicitness with which you need to go about this process is probably the only thing that makes special education "special."

By using yourself as an instrument,[1] some technical skill, a sensitivity to others, and a knowledge of a community and its resources, you can chart a sensible course and program.

Increased Public Interest in Special Education

Special educational services to handicapped children have a very brief history in this country. At about the same time that compulsory public school systems were being established, so were both private and public residential schools for the handicapped. Almost one hundred years ago, such residential schools served separate groups of handicapped: the blind, deaf, retarded, epileptic, and others. They provided both training and a protective environment for their special students for the duration of their lives.

With school systems not yet well established, the total child population of each school district still small, and few diagnostic or treatment procedures yet developed, local school systems did not begin to provide services until approximately sixty years ago. Typically, separate classes for various types of exceptionality were developed, often within a segregated school building or at least separate from the main activity areas. Children cared for in their own public school systems were usually those with one single handicap who were considered to be ready for education (e.g., toilet trained). The multiply handicapped and the severely retarded found no place in most public schools and continued to be sent to institutions.

Parents of children with handicaps began to band together in separate groups focused on a single handicap to make certain that their children received education and other services. Over the past thirty years, parent groups helped sponsor and lobby for legislation designed specifically for a categorical handicap. Sometimes parent groups ran their own preschool programs, much like parent cooperative nursery schools. In some instances, they were able to convince state legislatures to assume financial and administrative responsibility for these classes via departments of mental health, public health, or the like. During these early years it was usually necessary to label children's disabilities as a first step in admitting them to special programs. Those who had more than one handicap and those with only a mild degree of difficulty still fit nowhere very well.

---

[1]Arthur W. Combs, *The Professional Education of Teachers* (Boston: Allyn and Bacon, 1965), pp. 68–81.

Over the past ten years an extraordinary amount of activity has taken place in special education as parents began to take their concerns to court. The resultant court decisions have stimulated both state and federal legislation to reform how, where, when, and what special education services will be provided.

It is not possible to mention all the court action that has taken place. However, we have selected three court cases that have had important consequences. In 1967, the Hobson v. Hansen decision abolished the track system practiced by the District of Columbia school system. At a particular age, children were placed in separate tracks (e.g., college, business, trade school) and were destined to finish their school careers in those tracks. It was argued that such a procedure is unconstitutional because it indirectly discriminates against black as well as poor children.

In 1970, assessment procedures were challenged in Monterey County in California. Agreement was reached in litigation initiated in behalf of Chicano children who were labeled *educably mentally retarded* and placed in a special class. It was argued that cultural bias was used when intelligence tests were given in English rather than in the language of the home.

A class action suit was filed against the state of Pennsylvania in 1971 by PARC (Pennsylvania Association for Retarded Citizens) in behalf of thirteen retarded children. The state had argued that it had a right to exclude children who were not yet ready to benefit from the educational program that a school system was providing. The subsequent decision affirmed the right to an education for *all* citizens, including the severely/profoundly retarded and the multiply handicapped.

Federal legislation for the handicapped began in 1965 as a part of the Elementary and Secondary Education Act (P.L. 89–313). A portion of that bill provided federal support for the education of handicapped children in state-operated hospitals and institutions. In 1967, P.L. 89–750 established the Bureau for the Education of the Handicapped, one of four bureaus in the Office of Education.

The Education of the Handicapped Act (P.L. 91–230) was introduced and passed in 1970. Title VI-B provided program support to the states but also asked each state to formulate a plan for special education. Training monies were designated to state departments and universities by Title VI-D. At this time programs for children, as well as training for teachers, were almost entirely segregated by categorical handicaps. Title VI-C, the Handicapped Children's Early Education Program, specifically earmarked funds for model interdisciplinary educational programs for special needs preschoolers in both private and public agencies. New intervention programs for children from birth to five years old and support services for their parents were encouraged by this legislation.

As stipulated by P.L. 93–380 (1974), by July 1975 all states were to complete a plan indicating how and when they would be able to provide full educational services to handicapped children between the ages of three and twenty-one. P.L. 93–380 also required each state to adhere to due process when conducting individual assessment and educational planning proceedings. In addition, states were advised that all plans for children should aim toward using the *least restrictive environment* commensurate with a child's needs. In some states this has meant that children must be in integrated classrooms, and when possible, they must be educated in integrated buildings. As might be anticipated, trends in teacher education have paralleled the shift toward more integrated programs. Programs and certification for generic specialists have become prominent.

In late 1975 the All Handicapped Children's Act (P.L. 94–142) extended the right of free public education to all the handicapped. By September 1978 handicapped children between the ages of three and eighteen are to be covered; by 1980 coverage can be extended to age 21. The act also sets up a permanent instrument in the Bureau for the Education of the Handicapped to subsidize grants to the states at levels that could reach as high as three billion dollars per year by 1982. Federal allocations to the states will be set for each handicapped child served; an additional incentive will be given to the states for each handicapped child between the ages of three and five enrolled in a program.

In keeping with the attempts to integrate handicapped children with normal children as much as feasible, Congress passed P.L. 92–424 in 1972. It specified that all Head Start programs, in order to retain their funding, must enroll and serve handicapped children so that the handicapped make up approximately ten percent of the total population of young children served.

The results of federal legislation and court decisions have been dramatic in their effect on state and local school departments. For example, Massachusetts passed legislation in 1972 making each local school department responsible for programming for children with special needs from age three to twenty-one. Some features of Chapter 766 are: mandatory screening for preschoolers and entering kindergartners, formal assessment procedures for those children identified as having special needs, participation of parents in the process of the assessment and educational planning for their child, orderly steps for appealing or reviewing those decisions about which the school and parents cannot agree, and continuing pursuit of the goal of integration of special needs children into the normal classroom, as feasible. The question of how the public can afford these services and their procedural safeguards is as yet unanswered. To strive for the quality of programs that is the intent of this legislation is ambitious and worthy of all our efforts.

Whether mainstreaming or another reform will make a difference is a question that is hotly debated. Blatt answers by calling our attention to Itard's relationship to Victor, the "Wild Boy of Aveyron," and to Ann Sullivan's struggles with Helen Keller: "There was a human spirit who sought an understanding with itself and with the finite world. And there was a great teacher. Inevitably, there was the interaction. That's what mattered."[2]

---

[2]Burton Blatt, "Mainstreaming: Does it Matter?" *Exceptional Parent* 6, no. 1 (February 1976): 12.

Bibliography

Blatt, Burton. "Mainstreaming: Does It Matter?" *Exceptional Parent* 6, no. 1 (February 1976): 11–12.

Budoff, Milton. "Engendering Change in Special Education Practices." *Harvard Educational Review* 45, no. 4 (November 1975): 507–26.

Combs, Arthur W. *The Professional Education of Teachers.* Boston: Allyn and Bacon, 1965.

Dunn, Lloyd, ed. *Exceptional Children in the Schools.* 2d ed. New York: Holt, Rinehart and Winston, 1973.

Glasscote, Raymond; Fishman, Michael E.; Cass, Loretta; Brunt, Hal; Lasher, Miriam; Koret, Sydney; Provence, Sally; and Braun, Samuel. *Mental Health Programs for Preschool Children: A Field Study.* Washington, D.C.: Joint Information Service of the American Psychiatric Association and the National Association for Mental Health, 1974.

Goodman, Leroy V. "A Bill of Rights for the Handicapped." *American Education* 12, no. 5 (June 1976): 6–8.

Kirk, Samuel A. *Educating Exceptional Children.* 2d ed. Boston: Houghton Mifflin, 1972.

National Advisory Committee on the Handicapped. *The Unfinished Revolution: Education for the Handicapped.* Annual Report. Washington, D.C.: U.S. Government Printing Office, 1976.

Chapter Two

Creating a Healthy Learning Environment

A group of young children is best served when the emotional needs of both children and adults are recognized and planned for. We have found that Erikson's formulation of the sequential developmental stages in the life cycle is a helpful guide toward conceptualizing the design of such a classroom.[1] This framework assumes that all people, and preschoolers in particular, struggle to develop a sense of trust, autonomy, and initiative. The classroom and the adults who work in it must reflect some understanding of these three issues.

None of us ever completely resolves earlier and continuing struggles with trust, autonomy, and initiative. Because remnants of past experience are always available to us, present events may occasionally highlight bygone plights. Spend but a few days in the hospital to deal once again with having to rely totally on others for creature comforts. Who will tend to your needs? When and how will they take care of you? Such an experience can help us better comprehend young children's concerns about trust.

We as adults also strive to maintain some control over a portion of our lives. It's not uncommon to recognize our own sense of frustration when the boss or the bureaucracy places some unexpected demand on our work lives. After such encounters we may come home and begin to

---

[1]Erik H. Erikson, "Identity and the Life Cycle," in *Psychological Issues* 1, no. 1 (New York: International Universities Press, 1959), pp. 50–100.

pick on our mate. He or she, in turn, passes it on to the children, who end up tormenting the cat. Indeed, the toddler is not the only person who struggles to exercise autonomy!

Our daydreams are similar to a young child's experiences with initiative. We entertain fantasies of our potential or other alternatives available to us in our lives. At the height of a raging snowstorm with the prospect of shoveling our way out, we may well imagine spending the rest of our lives on the sandy beach of a tropical island. On other occasions we may have pictured ourselves having successfully played a romantic lead to an adoring audience.

You can better understand the preschoolers you work with if you can learn to tune in on your own struggles with these universal issues. Doing so will help you personalize and add to some of our suggestions about constructing a healthy emotional climate in the classroom. While a child described as having special needs can place a strain on any classroom, these children are not so unique. Attention to basic structure and function of a class is good for all children and will help to alleviate the strain. We include some examples of children who reminded their teachers to provide more explicitly, not just for one child's needs, but for the well-being of the whole class. By using such a formulation along with a developmental framework, you can identify activities and interventions that can benefit all children.

Later we will discuss some common problems that arise in preschool programs. For instance, teachers often attempt to solve classroom problems by adding more adult helpers. These additional bodies usually create more demands on a teacher's time and attention unless the teacher also makes adjustments in attitude and behavior. Another area of importance often overlooked concerns choosing children for a group and using peer subgroups for socialization purposes. We also highlight the separation experience for young children, since it is one of the most critical processes to which a teacher attends. Too frequently a teacher considers separation concerns to have been handled when a child is physically in a classroom without his parent and without an expression of negative feeling. Yet that may be only the beginning of a true resolution.

Building Trust

Building trust in a classroom is an exercise that allows children to learn to depend on people and the classroom environment. Children vary as to their need to have a predictable and reliable day, but they all need to have structure and people they can rely on. A relationship to nurturant adults is strengthened by the adults' consistent availability and capacity to provide a safe environment. Such a relationship, once established, can withstand uncertainty and strong emotions. The adults to whom children become attached demonstrate their caring by establishing routines as well as time and space boundaries.

In some classrooms the time schedule is an important element around which children learn to predict what comes next. They learn to pace their interests and activities throughout the day. In one class where the children were developmentally slow, the teachers needed to anticipate how long most children would stay with an activity. They observed that most children stayed with their chosen activity about ten minutes; consequently, they set a timer to ring a bell at ten-minute intervals during the hour-long activity period. This helped children anticipate that a new choice needed to be made. Using a timer to signal a structure to segments of the day may seem inflexible, and indeed it is. However, it served an important purpose for this group of children and their teachers. Highlighting the structure helped children begin to develop their own sense of timing.

Some classrooms need to define space and places to store or display materials within that space. Such preplanning is essential in an open classroom where demarcation of work areas rather than time schedules help define the day. Yet in any classroom, space for different activities must be well thought-out. A reading area may prove disastrous juxtaposed next to a block-building area. It works better to cushion a quiet space from a noisy place with vertical dividers, work tables, and sound-absorbing materials.

Some children need to have a carefully delineated work surface. Masking tape applied to a table top to mark individual work places may remind those with an exaggerated sense of territorial imperative. Colored place mats made from sheets of construction paper and covered by a large sheet of clear contact paper are another possibility. Some children are so distractable that they cannot share a work space at all without a tri-wall divider placed on the table top, reminiscent of a cubicle or library study carrel. Such a structure is easily fashioned by fitting together two separate pieces of cardboard with slots, making four individual work areas on a table top. One teacher of impulsive troubled four year olds used a similar technique to define individual floor spaces for block building and truck play. Made from tri-wall sections just four inches high, they surrounded the child and his materials on the floor.

The degree to which you improvise spatial structures to demarcate and accent space will depend on the characteristics of the children with whom you work: distractability, high activity level, inability to differentiate subtlety, oversensitivity to others. It is preferable to start by oversimplifying the environment. If you do not plan ahead, the children will force you to take action to help clarify the confusion.

Routines or transitions require careful thought before the children arrive, as each concrete detail can assume importance. Serving a snack is an example of an event of incredible complexity requiring many decisions. Some of those decisions are arbitrary; some involve values; still others communicate a set of specific expectations for children. In one program, for instance, the children did not participate in preparing for snack or cleaning up afterward. They were served by adults who waited on the tables, never taking seats themselves. Think of the number of questions this activity poses. Should children wash their hands before eating? Should they help distribute the cups and napkins and serve the juice or crackers? Should they have their own color-coded cups? Should their chairs be assigned? Should they pour their own juice? Should a child be required to ask in words before receiving seconds? Should they stay at the table until everyone is finished? Should they throw away their own disposable utensils?

Developing smooth routines and transitions takes forethought and considerable organization. It means anticipating to what extent children can read expectations from the environment without your constant attention. The availability of oilcloth smocks that slip easily over a child's head and their placement near the easel or water table make their usage clear after a few reminders. A receptacle visible near the juice table suggests that children will throw away their own cups and napkins.

Some children require that your *caregiving* be demonstrated concretely and individually. For many this moment inconveniently occurs at the start of the day when teachers are busy setting up and greeting children. Some children need breakfast and arrive hungry; others need their faces washed and hair combed. These simple acts of nurturance may be precisely what is needed. Not only does it cement your relationship, but it helps some children get organized for school. They otherwise might have wandered around school, dabbling at activities or striking out at others, disinterested and hungry.

It's a rare child who doesn't like a hug or some lap time from a teacher. However, children may also be able to fulfill one another's needs for nurturance. Lena, the third of five children six years old and younger, came to school smelling of urine, whining and clinging. Any adult within her vision soon received pleas to be held. Extricating themselves from her grasp entailed literally peeling her from their bodies. This four year old was easily introduced to the housekeeping corner, where she quickly assumed playing the role of the needy baby curled up in bed. Within a few minutes, her teacher introduced her to a series of would-be parents who tended to her complaints and pleadings. Because they legitimized her need to be a baby, she no longer needed to bootleg attention. It took two months before she gave up her demand to be treated as a baby, yet her classmates were willing to minister to her for seemingly as long as she needed.

Some children need concrete reminders of the people who care for them. A snapshot is one of the easiest ways to respond to such a need. If going from school to home is difficult for children, taking home a picture of themselves and their teacher in the classroom is often sufficient to help them tolerate the uncertainty introduced by the ending of each day. Such a technique has proven useful to children for whom home is an unpredictable place. Those having difficulty leaving home or saying good-bye at the end of the school year have also found a picture comforting.

So far we have been considering children who acknowledge the presence of others. But for children who might be called *withdrawn, psychotic,* or *severely communication disordered,* developing an effective working relationship requires the rigors of *behavior modification* techniques. These children do not consistently make eye contact with anyone; they do not come or attend when their names are called. These children should not be confused with those whose unresponsiveness is a result of a separation problem. Separation-related difficulties can be easily confirmed by observing the child's behavior at home, where he will appear comfortable and related to familiar adults.

The children we refer to are often psychotic and may be barraged with words as adults coax them to activities. Too frequently the attention itself merely prolongs the habit of not looking or not attending. We have found it wise to be predictable and reliable by consistently offering a reward (such as dry cereal, a morsel of cookie, or whatever the child finds desirable) when the child makes eye contact after his or her name is called (e.g., "Sheila, look"). Make certain that you are at her eye level, guiding her head in your direction if necessary. If a table is to be your work space, give your instructions from there to have more control of the variables. When the child complies, give the reward quickly and couple it with praise. Remember not to coax; you are trying to make your words meaningful and reliable. When the child behaves consistently, you may no longer need to give a material or edible reward.

A similar procedure should be followed when you take the next step: teaching the child to come when his or her name is called (e.g., "Tony, come here"). These children may also need to be taught to follow simple directions or to imitate the actions of others in activities. It is essential that you be able to describe the specific target behavior and be prepared to reward a series of approximations of the desired behavior. You must be certain about what is rewarding to the child and that those rewards are given promptly after he has performed the target behavior or an approximation of that behavior. "Relating to adults" is too general a goal. Making eye contact, coming when called, and following one-step directions are the early building blocks upon which relationships are formed.

Remember that the more often behaviors are followed by pleasant consequences, the more likely they are to reoccur. Your "fussing" or coaxing may never have occurred to you as a pleasant consequence to the inattentive child for *not* looking at you. Yet you may inadvertently find that the child who avoids eye contact is being rewarded for the very behavior you are trying to discourage.

The principles of behavior modification are elemental in building predictable and reliable working relationships with many children, especially those who lack basic skills in relating to others. They need to be able to attend when they are called and to imitate others as necessary first steps toward "learning to learn." The booklets by Baker et al.,[2] although written for parents, have served as a useful introduction to behavior modification for beginning teachers.

Sharing Autonomy

In the section on building trust we emphasized the need to set the stage for learning. Predictability and reliability were key ingredients that helped children learn to depend on people and their environment. Children also need to learn to make choices in the classroom. Choices help a child exercise his will and experience a sense of authority or independence. At the same time, adults who provide choices must be mindful that there are limits to the number of options some children can tolerate, especially if they have few inner controls.

For instance, it can be pointless, if not provocative, to fill the room with materials for children who have had few experiences with play materials. The children will end up playing with everything and nothing, and you will eventually be forced to take steps to control the environment. In the beginning, therefore, you will need to decide how many choices to offer.

---

[2]Bruce L. Baker et. al., *Early Self-Help Skills; Intermediate Self-Help Skills;* and *Behavior Problems* (Champaign, Ill.: Research Press, 1976).

Distractable children and children unaccustomed to making choices need to start in a stripped-down classroom. You can always add materials and decorations at a future date. Both you and the children need to feel in command of the classroom environment. You have a responsibility to limit the number of activities and play materials available according to what you feel is wise and safe enough for the class to handle. Most beginning teachers fear that there may not be enough materials, but such an attitude only courts chaos.

Children need to participate in making some of the decisions. The younger they are developmentally, the more narrow and circumscribed the choice: "Can you bring the chair to the table or shall I help you?" You are not really asking what he would like to do, but how the objective will be accomplished. Young children respond to such guidance. They don't like to receive orders any more than the rest of us.

Another way to avoid power struggles or chaos is to depersonalize rules: "What can we do? It's eleven o'clock and time to clean up!"; "We have to wait until juice and crackers before . . ." ; or "In school we don't hit or bite; we tell others what we don't like." The rules or code of the classroom are established over time so that they become shared by the children. In fact, most children who have been together for a length of time remind one another and newcomers about what the rules are. They feel that the rules are their own—a logical extension of a classroom where freedom and responsibility are shared.

Any discussion of choice, rules, controls, or willpower assumes that we have a sense of proportion or priority about what is important to insist on and what is not. Kelly felt it was important to keep her coat on. Her teacher agreed and told her so: "You know, Kelly, some things you're boss of and some things I'm boss of. I know it's important for you to boss your own coat. You can take it off when *you're* ready." It usually took about ten minutes for her to decide she wanted to discard her coat, that is, when she became too warm.

Using the word "boss" with young children helps legitimize their need to be in control or exercise their will. Fred had great difficulty approaching any paper and crayon task his teacher suggested, refusing both perfunctory and firm invitations of help. It was only when his teacher suggested showing him how to boss the crayon so that it would go where *he* wanted it to go that Fred accepted help. The struggle moved from his relationship to his teacher and the lesson to the real heart of the matter—his mastery of writing.

Jenny needed a well-defined work space of her own. Not only did it cut down on the amount of distraction, but her "office" was a place where people entered only when invited. It reminded her that she was the "boss" of what went on there (within reason), in contrast to other parts of the room where she was subjected to the will of others. Without such clear definition Jenny had remained in constant vigil, waiting for the slightest hint of a demand. The solution to her dilemma was reached after her teacher observed that much of her day was spent in tantrums and abrasive interactions; no learning had been taking place.

Some children do get out of control and need to be held for their own safety and the safety of others. During such an "exercise"—and it can be just that—refrain from trying to reason with the child. This is no time for a lucid discussion. Instead, think through how you might need to sit a child in a chair, criss-crossing his arms and holding them from behind the chair, mindful that your chin can be butted by a child's head. Only from such a position can you ensure your own safety and make your words meaningful: "I won't let you hurt anyone." You might anticipate how it feels to hold someone as he shouts claims that you are breaking his arm. The first tantrum raises every doubt you ever had about your own judgment and worth. Riding through a tantrum from beginning to end restores confidence to a beginner and is a true bench mark in your teaching career.

Most children are reassured to know that you can keep them safe and are not intimidated by their actions. Mark had been threatening children all morning. He started to swing a block, which grazed another child's head. When he was stopped, a scuffle ensued. His teacher told him that she would have to boss his body until he was able to boss it himself. They struggled in the chair as he kicked and spat, shouting that he was able to boss himself. She gently and firmly said he could show her he was in charge again when his body was relaxed. After fifteen minutes he looked up, managing a faint smile. Many children, having experienced your ability to take charge, will build an alliance with you and ask for help when they feel out of control.

Such experiences remind us of what a human profession guiding young children can be. After being provocatively kicked in the shins, you may miss the mark by bland cerebral remarks such as "You can tell me what you want another way" or "I like you, but not your kicking." It is better to give some honest feedback with feeling: "Ouch! That hurts. Stop kicking this minute!" Guiding children through their negativistic struggles entails physical work, as many children do not trust the meaning of words. It follows that they only respond to a teacher's verbalizations when accompanied or preceded by a physical reminder. By gently directing or nudging such a child toward an activity, your verbal invitation seconds later will have more meaning. Deciding when to distract by physically guiding, when to insist even though it means a struggle, and when to walk away from potential disaster is not easy. However, such learning comes from familiarity with the skilled use of your muscles and not from your tongue.

To handle most tantrums or dangerous behavior, first use physical restraint as has been described. During these occasions, be careful not to inadvertently confuse the issue by making eye contact, physically cuddling, or offering excessive verbal attention. Living through violent tantrums has developmental significance for young children. They learn that adults are not intimidated by their behavior or their anger and that they will not be abandoned. Equally important, children appreciate that their own strong feelings won't annihilate their own sense of self. There comes a time, however, when the behavior supported by adult attention no longer serves the purpose of furthering development. In such instances, "time out" is needed.

"Time out" is a term from the field of behavior modification, derived from the observation that the frequency of a behavior increases when pleasant consequences follow it. "Time out" defines a situation in which there is a withdrawal of human attention as a consequence of a behavior. Having a child sit in a cubby or a chair away from others or in a stimulus-free room with the dutch door closed for a few minutes may serve to extinguish provocative behavior.

We trust that you will not be confused by our eclecticism, switching from a psychoanalytic framework to a more behavioristic point of view. For yet another opinion, consider Montessori. She advocated treating disruptive behavior by isolating a child in the corner or insisting that the child hold her hand and follow her around the room. Wherever she had to be the child went, without her talking or attending to him. When he felt he was ready to return to his work, he told her and was free to go. Incorrigible behavior was dealt with by expulsion. Whatever the practitioner's persuasion, the important denominator is consistency and deliberateness in the approach to disruptive behavior. Children will then appreciate that they have choices and learn to control their own behavior.

Often issues of autonomy and trust are combined in the classroom. Such a situation occurred when a teacher mentioned that ten of the fifteen children in her class were either disturbed or disturbing. It did not take long to observe that fighting broke out periodically in different parts of the room and that few of the children actually played together. More revealing was their behavior at the painting easel. After completing their paintings, the children glanced shiftily around the room. Each child seemed to look for the safe moment when his or her painting could be taken down and hidden. Later, the children read in small groups on a blanket where they also shared a communal bowl of peanuts. The major task perceived by the children was not the storytelling, but how to get more peanuts than their neighbors. In this classroom there were no cubbies or designated places to keep belongings and possessions. Improvised shopping bags for each child later mitigated the suspiciousness and fighting. Apportioning the snack to individual containers for each child also kept the children from having to take matters into their own hands.

Guiding young children requires a delicate balance of *doing for* and *doing with*. No one so young likes to be left in the position of managing totally on his own.

Encouraging Initiative

Both adults and young children like to feel unique, to daydream, to imagine alternatives for themselves, and to satisfy their curiosity about natural phenomena. Young children's initiatives are often taken up with imagining what it is like to be grown-up. Their considerations can be fraught with anxiety, joy, disappointment, and elements of risk. In many cases, the romantic possibilities they entertain will have to wait until they are older or may never be possible.

The alternatives a young child perceives are most often expressed in play. Role playing is a common activity of young children. Any "house corner" is teeming with activity as children try their hand at parenting, housekeeping, and shopping. Such activity helped Lena, who needed nurturance. However, the consequences of young children's play are not always anticipated.

Leroy wanted to build an airplane. He found a partner to help him, and they worked very hard making an enormous block construction. Each day brought a new elaboration until finally it was time for Leroy to fly. His sadness and anger were very real to him when the plane never got off the ground. Because he wasn't very articulate, he lashed out at his teacher. It was important for her to comfort him and later remind him that he would have to grow older before he could build a plane that flies. From such painful experiences children learn to become "students"; they appreciate that wishing will not make it so and that learning requires skills.

For some children whose older brothers and sisters already attend school, attending a preschool program can be very disappointing. Jane's teacher didn't believe in workbooks or worksheets, but Jane did. For her the workbook was a way to play being a student.

Frequently four or five year olds decide that the last thing they need is a teacher. They fend off adult help as though they knew everything already. By allowing themselves to be taught, they must acknowledge their status as children. In the middle of the year Lynn began walking into her classroom, ignoring her teacher's greeting. She and another girl did their best to reject their teacher's suggestions for activities during the morning. As the weeks passed they became more bold by teasing younger children, openly defying classroom rules, and talking during group singing. In a sense, Lynn needed to be reminded she had a teacher. The best time for this reminder came at the beginning of the day when the teacher insisted that her greeting be acknowledged. For Lynn, it helped when her teacher gently held her while she said hello. Her teacher also mentioned that she did not like to be ignored; in fact, she said, "I saved some time at 10:15 to teach your letters and show you a new game." Without intervention such young children can become increasingly provocative and anxious. It's no favor to leave young children with the notion that they are running the class.

We have considered some of the more unique ways children play at being grown-up. Their role playing is often sustained by their peers and encompasses the issues of trust, autonomy, and initiative. One small group of young boys, who were having difficulty controlling themselves, spent three months playing traffic games. They used tricycles and made their own "roads," "signals," and "signs." One boy took his turn as police officer while the others practiced their brakes, pretended to have accidents, and jointly mapped out traffic patterns. The teacher needed only to add a prop or two, encourage order when necessary, or help one or two children deal with the others. This role for a teacher emphasizes the ability of young children to learn from one another so that the peer group can assume greater importance. The teacher learns to share responsibility with the group, helping children label and express their feelings appropriately and teaching them how to negotiate with others and to play cooperatively. The teacher's mere presence usually fosters these expectations for the group.

To further emphasize that children can help one another, the teacher learns to make their concerns a matter of "public record." A group of children may have common concerns: beginning the school year, a trip, a rainy day, a dead pet. They may not articulate these concerns in logical paragraphs or in an orderly group discussion. The group of boys who played traffic games were interested and worried about safety, controls, and bodily injury. Their play wove together common concerns and helped them master and talk about their behavior and feelings. They learned to appreciate that their feelings and behavior were related, but they did so in the context of playing games that appealed to their sense of romance about driving an auto. The teacher's ultimate goal was to help them connect their feelings of fear and anger to their acting-out behavior.

For developmentally younger children, just learning to play cooperatively is an achievement. The group activity must be less complex and demanding, in contrast to the romance of the aforementioned traffic games. Instead, the task for a younger group may be to learn to use interlocking train tracks and trains, where pooling resources works to everyone's benefit. The materials themselves make explicit their usage, and there are clear role expectations for the children involved. Children with fewer social skills obviously need more teacher intervention to facilitate group activities.

You can use the group in other ways. In addition to making common group concerns public, you may choose to make some of their individual problems public. You may speak about a child in front of that child by directly addressing classmates or another adult in the room: "Joe is shy. He's not used to making friends, but we can help him" or "Carla is worried today; maybe that's why it's so hard to share." After Frank has hit Joe in the shoulder, you may comfort Joe and tell him that Frank needs to hear the words, "Stop that; it hurts!" Mention that hitting is scary and may be scary for Frank as well. In this way, you can help children use words to express feelings and ideas so that members of the group can help one another.

You cannot work on problems of initiative with children without having anticipated or resolved how you will deal with the issues of autonomy and trust. Having done so, you set the stage and enforce the rules which permit a group of children to explore the possibilities they imagine for themselves and one another. When these possibilities stimulate feelings of anxiety, pleasure, anger, or sadness, the classroom can then allow those feelings to be expressed and shared.

Common Concerns

Beginning teachers often wonder how to decide on a group's composition, especially if they have a choice. Sometimes the question about whether to include a child with special needs is raised. There is no more complicated question, for you cannot accurately predict how children will behave at school. Usually, you can get some indication of their activity level, cognitive level, and emotional stability. Assuming you have such information, you can attempt to achieve a balance between active and quiet children. You should avoid too great a diversity in developmental level so there are some shared interests within the group. You will make some decisions on the basis of subtle factors, such as taking a physically small older child who is retarded and integrating him into a class of normal, chronologically younger children. Other decisions will be made on a highly personal basis, such as knowing that you like to work with aggressive, slow, or shy children. It is reassuringly human that these are the ways in which most classes are set up.

Unfortunately, classes are too often expected to be assembled too quickly. Some children might be better served by a later school entry date, especially if you expect discipline problems. Once routines and rules are shared by the children, you have allies in the class. They can be powerful socializing influences on entering students.

The most common request of any beginning teacher is for extra help in the classroom, although the consequences are usually not anticipated. The presence of more adults creates problems in human engineering. Two or more adults do not make a functioning team without work and planning. Since learning to communicate is a major key to teamwork, do not ask for volunteers in your classroom unless you are prepared to talk with them and to guide their activities.

A classroom which appears adequately staffed with a teacher and two aides can still make requests for more help. Too often the problem is related to lack of teamwork. The teacher complains that the adult helpers are lazy and do nothing unless told. At the same time the aides feel intimidated by the teacher who, from their perspective, "hogs the show" and knows what to do but never tells them what to do. These adults can work a whole year in the same classroom without knowing more than the stereotype they originally created for one another. Communication about their dissatisfaction could have helped build an atmosphere that encouraged teamwork.

It takes time for a team to function nonverbally so that a gesture from one adult is understood by others on the team. Until such time it's better to overtalk before, during, and after class. Children usually spur adults to talk during class. If a child is interested in determining if adults deal with him in a similar fashion, he may test each one in rapid succession. If the adults do not let one another know what has happened, they are behaving as if they are blind. Their different approaches to discipline and failure to communicate may also encourage later arguments among themselves. It helps for Rosa to hear her teacher, who helped settle a dispute between Rosa and a friend, tell another adult in a different part of the room what transpired as Rosa grouses toward the next adult.

Talking before and after class helps the adults set the stage, agree upon the rules, and plan curriculum and strategy. Begin by having each person mention something he or she liked that happened during the day. When bringing up problems, be specific about the behavior you are describing: its antecedents, its consequences, and your feelings about it. Don't let yourself or your teammates make general statements like: "Things went better today" or "Tina seemed in a better mood." Your observations and different perceptions are too valuable to be lost in generalizations or unexplained judgments. You need each other for validation of your own perceptions, but you also need each other for support.

A Common Goal

There is no more important achievement for a young child than the emotional mastery of leaving his parents and coming to school. Sometimes schools make no provision for the gradual introduction of children and families to their teachers, nor do they help children deal with their feelings about separation.

While visiting one such program on its first day, we observed the children wandering uncertainly and teachers stumbling valiantly to recall a child's name. The program was started without introductions and without gradualness. Only one child, Josie, looked as though she came full of good humor and eager to play with materials. By the time the table was prepared for lunch, several brave children burst into tears as if to suggest that school had gone on long enough and it was time to go home. One could imagine children envisioning an overnight stay! No one commented on the tears or their worries about coming to school. When this visitor turned to Josie to bring up the topic during lunch, many of the children looked relieved. Josie eagerly mentioned that she was not afraid of coming to school because she had come to school with Casper. Casper was not her father, brother, or uncle, but a friendly ghost who protected Josie from the scariness that lurked in the corners of the classroom. Even Josie, who was outwardly least affected by beginning school, was haunted by the separation experience.

Even with the best preparation, children may not easily adapt to school. They need a chance to share how they feel. A few struggle very quietly, obligingly bringing their bodies to school while their souls remain at home. Their behavior so expresses their reluctance that they appear deaf or psychotic because they do not respond to words or acknowledge anyone at school. At home they are entirely different. They need to know that their teacher realizes they are not sold on school yet and that they do not have to respond verbally. A reminder during a transition lets a child know that her teachers understand she will join the class when she has made up her mind, which may take weeks. Home visiting may help make her decision to come to school a little easier. She is trying bravely to deal with her feelings.

More typical is the heartfelt tug of a child who, frightened to leave his mother, insists that his mother come to school with him. Because he can express himself, he is easier to deal with. The mother may be even more ambivalent, as a decision to send a child to school is fraught with many unexpected feelings: losing her child, redefining herself as a mother, facing "middle age," feeling judged about her ability to raise children. This can be a time for uncertainty for mother, child, and teacher. Solutions tend to be extreme. Parents are not allowed to come to one school at all, while at another school the decision about when to leave is left completely up to the parents.

Many schools prefer to ask parents to stay a few days, if possible, and let the teacher take responsibility for effecting the separation. This may require holding a child or ushering a mother to the door. It is reassuring for children to know that you are responsible for what goes on at school. They may not like it, but children shouldn't be expected to decide to come to school and to enjoy leaving home at the same time. In like fashion, parents need to feel that you know what you're doing and that you have encountered tantrums or separation fears before. Since the beginning of the school year is a busy time for teachers, arrange a separate time to visit with parents. Don't try to listen to a parent at a time when listening is a problem for you.

Furman describes a boy whose reaction to nursery school entry was quite bland.[3] After several months he remained uninvolved and answered the teacher's questions in monosyllables. He expressed neither sadness, anxiety, nor anger at the start of school. He behaved as if the school didn't exist for him. After some help from his mother and teachers, he later expressed sadness and fear. The fear was expressed in dangerous play on a jungle gym in front of his teacher, which prompted her to remove him and say directly, "Jim, I think you're testing me to see if I'll keep you as safe at school as mother does at home." Anger was not expressed until some months later when his teachers noticed consistent lateness to school and his crankiness.

****

> The head teacher finally quite tactfully took up the lateness with the mother at the point when he was missing about half an hour at the start of each day. The mother then told of a most difficult night problem which had been going on for about two

[3]Robert A. Furman, "Experiences in Nursery School Consultation," *Young Children* 22, no. 2 (November 1966): 88.

months. Jim dawdled and delayed in going upstairs, in getting ready for his bath, in bathing, in getting on his pajamas and then, when finally in bed, would begin an interminable series of trips to the bathroom or downstairs to ask his mother or father rather tedious questions that could well have waited until the next day. Any gentle or firm insistence that he stop the nonsense and get into bed had been met with rather severe yelling, screaming temper outbursts.

The teacher at once recognized that his anger about leaving his mother to start school had been moved to home to make its appearance when he had to leave her to go to bed. The teacher chided the mother a bit for not having told her of this difficulty that, in timing, seemed so clearly connected with really working through his starting of school. The mother was rather confused and said she felt this had been a home problem that was hers to work out and could have had nothing to do with school since it had not occurred there. I rather doubt if the teacher would have chided her quite so much if she had not felt herself remiss for not asking about the appearance at home of the feelings, whose absence we had so directly noted and wondered about.

Mother Reassures Child

With but a little help from the teacher, after the original connection had been made, the mother was able to help Jim by pointing out that his angry feelings at bedtime had started just when they had begun to talk about his feelings about starting school, and that she felt he had been angry for weeks, not about leaving her to go to bed, but rather about leaving her to go to school. Jim listened her out very attentively before demanding, "Well, what do you do all morning at home with the baby?" The mother immediately took up his obvious feeling that she sent him away to school so she could stay all morning at home with his baby brother and assured him of how much she missed him and she sent him to school to get him ready for kindergarten so he could grow up to be the big school boy he so wanted to be.

The night disturbance did not stop in a night or a week, but did subside gradually over the course of the ensuing month. . . . Jim . . . reaffirmed . . . that there is a triad of feelings involved in separation and that we cannot feel the job has been accomplished until all three have come to the surface in whatever manner and at whatever time they choose. And sometimes, with a child with very rugged defenses, they do not make themselves apparent until even during a second year in school. . . . The feelings do not [always] show at school but rather at home where the mother either does not connect them with school or rather suffers them through or works them through without telling the teachers what has transpired. For teachers who do not want to see or know about separation feelings these particular mechanisms in mother and child make it possible for the unsightly never to be seen.

[After the summer] Jim had apparently eagerly returned to school. In fact he had been so eager and controllable and so much in love with his school that the teachers well recognized what was going on. On arriving in the mornings when his mother had done the driving, he rather rudely sent her on her way home, interrupting one day a conversation between his mother and teacher with, "Haven't you gone yet?" He scorned the newly starting children whose mothers were sometimes spending the morning at the school, helping their children to start. He was clearly the master of the situation now except that he was a rather cruelly bossing master, so often just curtly dismissing his mother. Only a few times did this behavior change, and at these times he would ask his mother's help with his coat or boots and then require many minutes of her help with tasks he could do on his own in a matter of seconds.

But the real difficulty came at the end of the day, when Jim kept his mother waiting forever while he finished this project or that one, or took forever getting on his coat. When she would urge him to hurry up he would become cross with her or would explain how much fun he was having at school or how much he enjoyed it and hated to leave.

The teachers recognized this collection of defenses very well and it seemed to them that Jim was having separation trouble again. They were very familiar with the child who turns it all around, who is not left in the morning by his mother but rather works it out so that he leaves her; the child who does not wait all morning for his mother to come but rather makes her wait for him at the end of the school session; the child who is not missing his home and beloved mother but rather only has some trouble in leaving his beloved school and teachers. . . . [4]

****

[4]Ibid., pp. 89–91. Reprinted by permission from *Young Children,* Vol. XXII, No. 2 (November 1966), pp. 89–91. Copyright © 1966, National Association for the Education of Young Children, 1834 Connecticut Ave. N.W., Washington, D.C. 20009.

Summary

Building an emotional climate in the classroom is really predicated on your being in touch with the child who resides inside you. That child is there because you, too, were a child once. Your understanding of young children will be enriched by claiming that part of yourself. Your ability to plan meaningfully for young children will also be enhanced.

There are many ways in which adults differ from young children. The one we might well emphasize is the fact that we are politically more powerful. Children depend on us for many things. At best we are benevolent dictators in the classroom, willing to share increasing degrees of freedom and responsibility. By using a developmental framework and our own experiences as guides, we can truly build a classroom that nurtures and supports, offers choices within limits, and promotes initiative. Young children deserve our best efforts.

Bibliography

Baker, Bruce L.; Brightman, Alan J.; Heifetz, Louis J.; and Murphy, Diane. *Early Self-Help Skills*. Champaign, Ill.: Research Press, 1976.

———. *Intermediate Self-Help Skills*. Champaign, Ill.: Research Press, 1976.

———. *Behavior Problems*. Champaign, Ill.: Research Press, 1976.

Bensberg, Gerald J. *Teaching the Mentally Retarded*. Atlanta: Southern Regional Education Board, 1965.

Erikson, Erik H. "Identity and the Life Cycle." In *Psychological Issues* 1, no. 1. New York: International Universities Press, 1959.

Furman, Robert A. "Experiences in Nursery School Consultation." *Young Children* 22, no. 2 (November 1966): 84–95.

Furman, Robert A., and Katan, Anny, eds. *The Therapeutic Nursery School*. New York: International Universities Press, 1969.

Klein, Donald C., and Ross, Ann. "Kindergarten Entry: a Study of Role Transition." In *Orthopsychiatry and the School,* edited by Morris Krugman. New York: American Orthopsychiatric Association, 1958.

Mattick, Ilse. "Nursery School Adaptations and Techniques." In *The Drifters,* edited by Eleanor Pavenstedt. Boston: Little, Brown, 1967.

Murphy, Lois B., and Leeper, Ethel M. *Caring for Children: Away From Bedlam*. DHEW publication no. (OCD) 72–18. Washington, D.C.: U.S. Department of Health, Education and Welfare, 1970.

Osmon, Fred Linn. *Patterns for Designing Children's Centers*. New York: Educational Facilities Laboratories, 1971.

Rhodes, William C. "Curriculum and Disordered Behavior." *Exceptional Children* 30 (October 1963): 61–66.

Spivack, George, and Shure, Myrna B. *Social Adjustment of Young Children*. San Francisco: Jossey-Bass, 1974.

Trieschman, Albert E.; Whittaker, James K.; and Brendtro, Larry K. *The Other 23 Hours*. Chicago: Aldine Publishing, 1969.

Washburn, Ruth Wendell. "Re-education in a Nursery Group: A Study in Clinical Psychology." In *Monographs of the Society for Research in Child Development* 9, no. 2. Society for Research in Child Development, 1944.

Werlin, Kathryn. "Classroom Dynamics: Preschool Communication and Structure." *Teaching Exceptional Children,* 2, no. 1 (Fall 1969): 2–12.

Chapter Three

Looking Beyond Disturbed Behavior

Young children often behave in ways that puzzle adults. Lacking sophistication and words, they cannot easily let us know what "hurts" or when learning is difficult. Adults who care for young children are often left to play a variant of "twenty questions" in which a number of different hypotheses must be tested to isolate the child's difficulty.

In this chapter, we will look at some informal ways to assess the behavior of young children in regular as well as special educational settings. We will attempt to demonstrate that observations made by a teacher in group situations are clinically useful. Accurate observation can help outline a child's developmental profile and define appropriate educational programming and intervention.

Unfortunately, young children are most difficult to size up. They are the most vulnerable to upsetting family situations and crises. These transitory emotional upsets may influence a child's typical behavior, making it difficult to assess the extent or the existence of underlying learning problems. In addition, very young children have few words to convey "what's wrong." Even worse, they are slow to relate to strangers in unfamiliar surroundings. Anyone outside the familiar school or home setting will have a hard time getting started on an assessment process.

Yet uneasy teachers and parents often bring a young child to an "expert" in an office without first using their own resources to assess a child's strengths and weaknesses. In many instances, the physician or psychologist cannot make a definitive statement about what is wrong or whether to be worried at all. They may well send a distraught family away with instructions to relax and stop worrying, even though they share the concern that something may be wrong. Knowing the importance of comparing observations over time in charting a child's progress or lack of it, they elect to reassure a family rather than to raise their anxiety any further. Others may feel that nothing can be done at such a young age.

Teachers can be especially helpful in exploring parental concerns and doubts about a child's competence. Teachers see children in what are sometimes more comfortable, natural settings; they also have an opportunity to get acquainted with both child and family over time, in contrast to the physician or psychologist who must use standardized tools in a brief office visit or two. Teachers would be wise to pause with parents to gather observations and examine what they already know about a child. Those observations can be invaluable when other professionals are called upon to make a judgment about the nature of a disorder. This chapter is about systematic, yet informal ways to gather such observations.

Negativism, tantrums, refusal to try tasks, overdependence on an adult, aggressiveness, and excessive activity level are all familiar to any adult who works with "emotionally disturbed" children. Sometimes adults are too quick to conclude that a problem is interpersonal in nature; therefore, they are too ready to address themselves exclusively to feelings and family dynamics. However, these same behavior problems frequently conceal an underlying deficit in the child's learning abilities. When the secondary behavioral reactions are resolved, such children turn out to have a significant "learning disability"; that is, they have trouble translating sensory and perceptual input into symbolic form, remembering these symbols, or directing their bodies to use them appropriately. Other children can turn out to have a moderate degree of retardation or a deficit in auditory or visual acuity. In fact, there may have been many clues to the primary problem in their behavior. The lack of detailed observations and failure to place the data in a developmental framework make accurate assessment difficult.

Assessing Young Children in Groups

It is possible to observe some kinds of behavior in groups that are difficult to elicit in an individual relationship with an adult in an office.

The data you collect in a group about a child's social and emotional status is valid in relationship to his or her classroom functioning with teachers and peers. Data about cognitive performance illustrates a child's ability to attend to tasks in the midst of the normal confusion of a classroom environment. When a psychologist tests a distractable child in a quiet, simply furnished office, the child may function above his normal classroom performance level. A child may pass a standardized test given by a speech pathologist, yet he may have major difficulty making himself understood among peers in a classroom.

To do a thorough job of assessment in a classroom, teachers need a large mental catalog of tasks and activities which they can quickly assemble or improvise for use in situations that call on a child's natural interest in play and games. Equally important, they need a framework for organizing the data they collect which emphasizes a thorough knowledge of the normal developmental sequence.

Teachers who are responsible for children's education are not just interested in whether or not a child can perform certain tasks. They are concerned with his or her continued learning and progress. With informal assessment methods they can pose a series of "questions" to a child, whose "answers" become the behavioral response to particular tasks and situations and help the teacher accurately place that behavior along a developmental profile or scale.

Data placed in a developmental framework can also be used as a curriculum guide. For instance, a child who pulls himself to stand and cruises along the edges of tables and chairs, balancing himself with one hand, could be a "severely retarded" four year old or a "normal" twelve month old. No matter what his chronological age may be, the behavior is *developmentally* familiar; that is, children between ten and fourteen months do that sort of thing. If you think about children ten to fourteen months old whom you have known, the next step is obvious. This is a child who is ready to take his first uncertain steps without support. To encourage him to venture forth, he needs a physically safe environment and a person available to kneel down with arms held out to him. When he does take his first step, he needs social reinforcement for his accomplishments from someone who can recognize that for the next few weeks nothing may be as interesting to him as practicing and perfecting this new skill.

Assess a six-year-old child whose body is physically normal in size and leads you toward certain behavioral objectives. Constantly testing out whether you mean what you say, he or she says no in words and behavior to any suggestion, almost without listening to what you have asked. No matter what his chronological age or developmental quotient, he is a toddler repeatedly testing his strength and your capacity to follow through. From your observations, the approach to him is clear. You do not politely invite a toddler to join activities, nor do you turn him loose in an "open" classroom. Give him limited choices by saying, "Will it be puzzles or crayons now?" or "Will you put your coat on yourself or shall I help you?"

These examples demonstrate the importance of making behavioral observations that place a child accurately on a developmental continuum. Once this is done, questions about appropriate programming will be relatively easy to answer.

A Framework for Recording Observations

In this section we will suggest a way of gathering observations about an individual child in a group. We offer an outline to help organize a report about a child of preschool age. Under each heading are suggestions for materials and methods of gathering the observations. We have purposely kept the outline informal because we want to break away from the "mystique" of a formalized test. You can gather many observations during a child's spontaneous activity. Sometimes you must stage an activity or present some specific tasks to one or more children at a time.

Let's start out assuming you have some minimal information with which to begin. Above all, you should know the child's chronological age in years and months. (It is not sufficient to know that the child is "four." There is a vast difference between being "just four" and "going on five.") You should also know something about the child's family situation and their living and economic conditions. The number of brothers and sisters, prior school experience, and experiences with other caregivers are important facts. Naturally, you should attempt a brief statement about the kinds of difficulties the child has been having. With this information to refer to, observation begins.

When you gather data, pay attention not only to what the child does but to how he does it. Make some general statements about the degree of enthusiasm or caution with which he or she goes about his work. Does this vary according to the type of task requested? What reaction does the child show to failure? What happens if you insist that he repeat a task? Does silliness, negativism, excessive motor activity, or an elaborate discourse always result after a request to work with paper and pencil, for instance? Such patterns of behavior, important in themselves, may also be a clue pointing to the area of performance where the child has difficulty.

How long is his attention span for different types of activity? What about distractability or unnecessary body movement while working? You will notice some children who seem absorbed and even quite proficient in their work, yet their fingers or feet never stop moving while they work. Others are distracted by auditory or visual stimuli that interfere with performance. Would the child be equally successful in a small, quiet room and in a normally noisy classroom? Can he work as well at a table with others as he does seated alone at a small table facing the wall?

Can the child heed a warning that an activity is almost over? Is he able to leave his work, put things away, accept that it may not yet be finished or perfect, and move easily to another task? Keep these questions in mind as you read through the following sections on specific observations. The answers will help to define the type of learning environment or approach that best suits a child's learning style.

Introductory Statement

Make an initial comment about the setting in which the child is being observed: the time span, the adults present, the number and age range of other children present, the child's familiarity with the classroom and materials. Here is the place for comments about anything which especially influences your observation: the child had a cold, was reluctant to leave his caregiver, came late into a group that was in full swing, and so forth. You are simply setting the scene so that the reader can share the context in which your report was made.

General Appearance

Capture the child in a word portrait for someone who has not met him or her. Note the characteristics that immediately impress you when meeting him for the first time. How does he appear physically? How is he dressed? Some children are not clad appropriately for the weather; others wear garments that need too much adult supervision and impede independence. Is there anything unique about him? Is there a physical resemblance to either parent? This is important because you will occasionally find that what appears to be a physical defect, odd mannerism, or defective speech pattern is simply a good replica of a strong family characteristic. Notice anything striking about the child's pace or activity level. Does he appear as a child of his stated age? It is an important diagnostic clue when everything in your description hangs together for a two year old, but you are talking about someone who is chronologically 3½.

Separation from Mother or Other Caregiver

You may be observing this child in an ongoing preschool group to which he or she is already fully adjusted. But separation from parents or important figures (including teachers) provides a particularly revealing moment to observe his manner of leaving an important relationship and starting or resuming another. His way of doing so may well be repeated each time he comes and goes from school albeit in a less elaborate or emotionally charged fashion. Comment on his reaction: crying, withdrawal, tantrums, denial, quick but premature attachment to another person. In relation to other children his age, evaluate the ease with which he manages this important transition.

Speech, Language, and Communication

A child's capacity to communicate effectively in words will greatly influence his or her family relationships, success with peers, and learning in school. His skill in expressing himself reveals a lot about his constitutional makeup, intellect, and emotions and gives important diagnostic clues to the problems he is having. You should develop shorthand methods to quickly and accurately record the things children say, including their sentence structure and content and the errors they make in pronouncing sounds in words. Unless you keep pencil and paper handy, you will have difficulty recalling specific responses.

This section of your report needs subheadings to help organize your findings. Begin with the child's *speech*—the technical ability to produce sounds and words. First note *vocabulary*. What is the basic fund of words the child has at his disposal? Are all the various parts of speech represented, or is his speech confined to crucial content words found in the beginning labeling vocabulary of a two year old? Can he learn new words when given exposure and practice with objects and experiences in school? Picture dictionaries and lotto games are good tools for assessing basic vocabulary. Ask the child to identify, by pointing, things you name (receptive vocabulary). Later ask him to tell you the name of something when you ask, "What's this?" (expressive vocabulary). Record his spontaneous language during a ten-minute supervised but unstructured play period. Go back over your recording and note the variety of words and parts of speech used.

Listen to *articulation*—the clarity of sound production—while assessing vocabulary. Be aware of a developmental progression in a child's production of sounds. Young children first master vowel sounds and the consonant sounds made with the lips, tongue, and teeth at the front of the mouth, such as *m, d, b, p, t*. Difficult sounds such as *f, s, v* and blends such as *th, br, sl,* and *bl* are mastered much later, sometimes not until a child is six years old.

It takes an acute ear to hear the errors a child makes and a ready pencil to jot them down. The job will be easier if you are systematic. Use standard picture cards or sentences which contain particular sounds you want to test; they will help you remember the errors that are made. Make a set of picture vocabulary cards of objects in which the key sounds are either at the beginning, the middle, or the end of words. Listen to the *b* sound in "bed," "table," "crib" and the *d* sound in "doll," "radio," "hand." You may discover the child can always pronounce the sound at the beginning of one-syllable words but usually has trouble combining it with another consonant in the middle of a word. That discovery is a sophisticated observation of the type a speech clinician would make, and it allows you to compare the nature of the error with the rest of the child's developmental profile to see if there is a discrepancy. Articulation errors are more likely to occur when a child is tired, hurried, or tense; therefore, the setting and emotional climate in which you observe should be described in your report.

When you have made these observations about speech, you are ready to think about *language*—the ability to put words and ideas together in a conversational exchange for which one must attend, listen, understand, and produce an appropriate spontaneous response. This capacity to receive, process, and express language is important for the child's later, more academic learning. By the time a child is six or seven years old, language works easily as a tool to learn about the world and to communicate with others.

Observations of a child's language can be divided into two major categories. *Receptive language* refers to what the child can take in, understand, and act on. Developmentally it comes first. Anyone who has observed toddlers knows that they understand many things they cannot yet speak about. Receptive language taps the store of words and concepts a child has been able to put away in his memory for future use.

To assess receptive language skills, you can again ask a child to identify pictures of objects or to point to real things around the classroom. In addition, give some verbal directions without any gestures. Just because a child may learn the routine of a classroom and seem to understand things does not mean he knows *words*. In fact, he may be getting few clues from words themselves. If he has heard "Put your things in your cubby and get ready for juice" day after day, he need only pick up one key word such as "cubby" or "juice." From experience and social context he will fill in the blanks. At another time and place, however, he would look confused when you used a sentence of equal complexity if there were no further clues to help him.

When you are satisfied that the child has a real understanding of the words he hears, start to observe for *expressive language*—the capacity to withdraw words from storage, put sentences together, and emit them spontaneously. You might play a game in which you and the child take turns labeling or describing pictures or asking questions that must be answered. Notice the child's language productions in spontaneous play where he may feel freer than in structured games. Listen for any differences that occur when he talks to his parents at the beginning or the end of the day. Children experiencing separation problems may talk little or very poorly in school, yet they chatter freely to their parents about school.

Be especially aware of the quality of the child's language production. If you ask a question such as "What's in the box?" his one-word response—"blocks"—may seem satisfactory at that moment. But if you show him a plate of carrot sticks and cheese cubes at snack time and ask what he would like, his pointing finger and one-word response—"that"—is qualitatively poor, leaving the responsibility for translation on the listener's shoulders. If you accumulate observations and realize that a four year old uses only one- and two-word phrases accompanied by gestures, you have discovered something significant.

Also notice any differences between a child's ability to talk about objects that are present and ideas or experiences that are removed from the "here and now." Sometimes a child can express himself when there are concrete referents present to look at or touch but cannot find the language to describe toys at home, what he had for breakfast this morning, or an experience over the past weekend. Such a child may have an expressive language difficulty. He relies on visual and kinesthetic cues as prompts to help him compensate for a weakness. Differences between receptive and expressive language skills are worth noting. In two and three year olds some lag in expressive language is developmentally appropriate, but a marked discrepancy or a lag that persists beyond age three may suggest a problem area.

When a child seems to have problems in the language area, try to isolate his skills in *auditory memory*. Ask him to repeat a series of spoken numbers that are not in sequence, such as "two, seven, five." By the time a child is about five, he should be able to repeat four or five digits. You may also assess his memory for sentences of meaningful material and for lists of unrelated words such as "boats, cats, apples, chairs." If he has difficulty with these tasks yet behaves age-appropriately in other respects, you have distinguished a language problem from a more generalized developmental lag.

Receptive and expressive language problems are often at the root of behavior that is sometimes confused with deafness, retardation, emotional disturbance, or even psychosis. When a child has trouble receiving language concepts or storing and retrieving them from memory for later use, he experiences a great deal of frustration. He may appear withdrawn, confused, untrusting, and unrelated to people and may actively fight, disrupt, or run away from situations he thinks will be too demanding or unsatisfying. A teacher observing him in a familiar natural setting has a good opportunity to notice his true abilities, the kinds of cues he relies on, and the kinds of help he needs in order to function. A child may behave age-appropriately when he can watch your face and gestures, when there is a familiar routine, or when things are slow and quiet. However, that same child may function poorly in the noisy bustle of a classroom, look confused, and seem to stare at your face for cues. Such a child may be deaf or have a communication disorder, but he is probably not retarded or psychotic.

A deaf child relies on visual cues, gets easily frustrated, and usually relates enthusiastically with a lot of bodily expression in situations where nonverbal communication can suffice. A psychotic child appears unrelated to people, uses objects in stereotyped ways, and may display self-stimulating or self-destructive behavior such as body rocking or head banging. A retarded child does not behave age-appropriately in any category of behavior but may relate well to people in the manner of a child chronologically younger. Discrepancies between language skills and other areas of behavior provide important differential diagnostic clues.

Gross Motor Development

Children need to be able to rely on their bodies to get them places and accomplish tasks. Children who are not sure they can control their muscles will feel insecure in many situations and may withdraw rather than become involved. Coordination problems and perceptual problems often combine to produce subsequent learning difficulties. In school you can observe motor coordination in spontaneous situations as well as in easily engineered activities. Note the overall degree of skill and comfort with which the child uses his or her body. Is he willing to try new things that involve perfecting skills in jumping and climbing, or is he content to sit at quiet table activities while others are active?

Are these choices a matter of interest and personal preference, or is he actively avoiding things he cannot do? Watch the way a child walks. Is his gait wide-based like that of a toddler, so that walking across a doorsill or rough surface still requires concentration? Or can he move with confidence, swinging his arms in rhythm as he goes and adapting to obstacles in his path?

Observe the child on stairs, which are particularly telling. Here again is a developmental progression that can easily be observed. A child of just two usually needs help on stairs. By 2½ he can go both up and down stairs, holding onto someone's hand or railing and using "parallel steppage" (both feet contacting each step). At three he can alternate feet going upstairs (one foot to each step) but still goes down in parallel fashion. By four to 4½ he goes easily up and down, alternating feet, with no need to hold on.

Some other gross motor landmarks to watch for are the ability to balance on one foot for a few seconds, to hop one or two steps on one foot, and to "lame duck skip" with one foot hopping, one foot walking; all these skills emerge at about four years. By five, one expects true skipping and greater proficiency in the other skills mentioned.

In relation to gross motor development, you should observe *laterality* and *directionality* for clues to later learning problems. An awareness of sidedness in his own body and the ability to use his side or limb in a refined and differentiated way are necessary for a child to smoothly perform many activities. Find out whether the child knows his right from his left hand, whether he is aware which hand he prefers for certain activities, and whether he uses one hand more skillfully than the other. Handedness is usually established by around four, though not always. The child may do some simple, well-practiced tasks such as pouring juice with the hand most convenient at the time, but he will always eat or write with the same hand once the preference has been established.

A child's ability to observe you as a model and imitate your movements is another useful clue to his sense of organization within his own body. Can he copy symmetrical movements of both arms in a game of "Simon says"? Can he move just one arm in imitation of you while the other remains relaxed at his side? By the age of five or six he should be reasonably proficient at such a game. He should not have to look at his own limbs to check where they are nor concentrate intensely as he watches you.

Skills with a ball are also worth observing. A three year old can catch a ball about eight inches in diameter with outstretched arms if you have aimed it gently and carefully; he can throw it back in your direction without tipping off balance, releasing it at the proper moment. A four year old can catch a smaller ball; if it is made of soft material such as styrofoam, he can grasp it in one hand and throw it back to you overhand. He will kick a ball rolled to him, adjusting his body to meet the ball with his preferred foot. Note whether he uses the hand and foot on the same side of his body. You can assess laterality further by noting which eye a child prefers. Roll up a piece of paper to make a telescope and play a "sea captain" game in which you take turns spying at each other. The eye he uses usually matches hand and foot preference.

Bumping into things, stumbling over other people's play materials, or spilling water in the housekeeping corner are signs of poor coordination and balance. Set up an obstacle course of boards, boxes, cardboard tubes, and a table large enough for a child to crawl under. Can he easily fit his body into these spaces without bumping himself?

Remember that you are looking for a whole collection of clues; no single failure should be considered highly significant. Your informal observations will help you decide whether there are real difficulties.

Fine Motor and Perceptual Motor Development

In school and in everyday life a child has to manipulate many tools: pencils, spoons, scissors, buttons, and shoe laces. His or her *fine motor* skills—the capacity to use small muscles with precision—are very important. In the first two years of life a child changes from someone who moves one whole side of his body, reaching for objects in gross fashion, to a more differentiated creature who can delicately oppose thumb and forefinger to pick up and release one tiny object among many. By the age of 2½ he can place six or seven one-inch wooden cubes on top of each other, and by three years he can build a tower of ten cubes before it falls. A three year old strings half-inch beads and begins to cut with scissors. By four he grasps a pencil as adults do, and by five he ties a knot.

Most observations of fine motor development also involve *perceptual motor* skills. The child must match *percepts*—what he sees or hears and is able to recognize and remember—with the ability of his hands and fingers to execute the task. To stack cubes he needs not only the skill to pick up and release the cube, but the ability to see the growing tower, place it in space, and control his hand movements precisely. Many school tasks involve this combination of motor skills with perceptual and conceptual information. A task that tests perceptual motor development is "copy forms," in which the child is asked to copy a geometric shape when shown a picture of it. Before the age of two, a child will imitate a simple vertical line after watching you make one. By three he copies a circle without seeing you draw one. By four he copies a cross; by 4½, a square; and by five, a triangle.

If a child cannot copy predrawn shapes, note whether observing you as you draw proves helpful to him. Does he need to hear you verbalize the motions as you draw? (A square is "down, over, down, over.") Observe a child's response as you try these various coaching techniques. This nets you a great deal more information than just a simple statement about what he can or cannot do, which is one reason why informal observations are so useful. When giving a formal test a psychologist is usually under severe constraints as to how a particular test item may be presented, what may be said, how the child's questions may be answered, and whether he may have any clues, coaching, or a chance for a second try. In informal teacher assessment you are not bound in the same way. You are interested not only in what the child can do but also in his style of approach. Most of all you want to discover whether any particular type of *coaching* is useful. Such additional information about a child with learning weaknesses will be especially helpful in making a "diagnosis" and planning for his "treatment."

One-inch colored wooden cubes, available from most school supply companies, are very useful materials for assessment purposes. Use about two dozen cubes, of which twelve or fifteen are of one primary color and the rest represent several assorted basic colors. There should be two or three cubes of each basic color. In the building tasks, use cubes that are all one color. This way the child's attention will not be distracted by color when you mean to focus on structure. If you help him start, will he build a tower? How many cubes high will it be before it falls? Is he aware of what is needed to make it straight and steady? How does he react when it falls? Can he imitate structures that you build, such as a simple bridge with three cubes or a set of stairs with six cubes? Here is another place where you can observe his response to coaching techniques. If a structure is shown for a few seconds and then hidden, can he reproduce it from memory? Does he need to see you go through the process of building it, hear you describe how it's done, or watch you count the blocks and verbalize their relationship to each other? Does he build as you build, placing each block as you place yours?

When asking the child to copy geometric shapes or inch-cube constructions, start by presenting a completed model he has not seen you build. Show it to him for a few seconds, then break it down and give him the same blocks to build with. Do not have any other blocks in view. If he cannot then reproduce what he had seen, you have a chance to discover something about his learning style. You can back up systematically through a series of coaching techniques, giving more help and making the task progressively easier until you find a point at which he is successful. But if you started off by letting him see you construct the model or by talking about how you did it, you will never know what his best performance could have been nor, on the other hand, how much help he may need. You could not test his memory and ability to motorically plan that particular task on his own.

Puzzles also help assess a child's perceptual motor skill and learning style. Puzzles vary greatly in type and complexity, from a simple homemade one of a single circular piece with a handle to interlocking puzzles with fifteen or twenty pieces whose shapes have no relationship to the picture being constructed. Notice a child's manner of approaching the task. Does he first dump all the pieces out and carefully turn them over to show the colored side, indicating he has experienced puzzles before and learned an orderly routine? Or does he search randomly, repeating the same mistakes and indicating that he has not begun to conceptualize what he is trying to piece together? Notice whether he responds mainly to color or to shape or whether he uses both attributes in deciding where a piece belongs. Must he try out each piece motorically to determine where it fits, or does he solve the problem with his eyes, making a thorough visual search before picking up the right piece?

Some children can see exactly where a puzzle piece should go but cannot orient it correctly to the available space; they seem to have trouble translating the visual information into motor movements. If this is true, see whether verbal coaching ("Turn the piece around") is helpful. Some children need to watch you trace the outline of the shape with your index finger and hear you verbalize "This piece has a big bump right here on the top. Let's find a hole with a bump on top just like that" before they can make the connection between what their eyes have seen and what their hands must do. Others just need some verbal cues about organizing the problem: "First let's find all the pieces that have some yellow on them for the school bus in the picture" or "This man needs another shoe down here at the bottom; can you find one more black shoe piece?" As you assess what kind of help is needed, you are teaching a useful method of approach to future puzzles. The chosen approach will have transfer value into more purely academic tasks such as recognizing letters and learning to read.

Cognitive Development

In this section you will be assessing the child's *knowledge*—the ability to combine skills with his hands, his perception of the world, and his stored language experiences to conceptualize or represent objects, events, and experiences. Children who are deaf, brain-injured, or for any reason are unable to develop spoken language have a more difficult struggle learning abstract concepts. Anything they cannot see, touch, taste, or smell is difficult to comprehend in thought. In this section, be aware that the tasks we present often assume that children have developed language labels and concepts which help them store their accumulated knowledge. Always bear in mind that when a child appears to fail at any task or activity or is unable to advance to a new stage of development, your task as an evaluator has just begun. You may have to test several different hunches or hypotheses before you feel satisfied to state what the difficulty is. You must find different ways to "ask" the same question about what the child knows so that a child who has difficulty in one modality or with one part of his body can still understand you and use what works best for him to "answer" you. This is critical insofar as conceptual development is concerned. When assessing young special needs children, you may have to learn to avoid using spoken language before it is safe to assume what a child truly does not "know."

To find out what a child knows you must also distinguish between things he has learned by rote and the concepts he uses to solve problems. Many young children "know their ABCs." They have learned the familiar rhyming sound or the sequence of letters by rote, but if stopped in the middle of either sequence, they have to start over again at the beginning. The letters themselves may have no significance and cannot be recombined to make meaningful units (words). Such rote skills are often cited by parents to demonstrate how bright a small child is. You must go beyond the rote skill to find out what the child conceptualizes about his world.

Assessment of *classification skills* can be a useful first step. If you present the child with a collection of miniature objects or picture cards of many objects, can he tell or show you "the ones we eat," "the ones we eat with," "the ones we wear," "the ones we ride in," and so forth? If so, can he name the general category such as food or clothing?

Concepts of color, shape, size, and number are basic to progress in academic learning. One-inch colored cubes are useful, as are attribute cards. Attribute cards are easily made from red, yellow, blue, and green cardboard. Make two complete sets of shapes—square, circle, triangle, and diamond—to include one large and one small shape of each color in each set. You now have cards that vary in three attributes: size, shape, and color. With these you can play a limitless number of sorting and classifying games that are usually quite appealing to children. With the youngest, put out two different shapes of the same size and color. Ask the child to find another shape "just the same as this" or "different from this." Note that you are not asking him to label the concept but to be able to recognize similarities or differences. (Remember that should he fail, you need to devise a way to find out whether he has understood the concepts "same" and "different.")

As you play this game, vary the size or shape or color while keeping the other attributes constant. The game can become increasingly more complex until you are varying all three attributes simultaneously and introducing more elements to deal with: "Find all the round ones; all the small ones; all the big red ones; all the ones that are not square; all the ones that are neither blue nor a triangle." You are assessing the child's ability to manipulate several factors, which is more complicated than merely knowing the individual concept labels.

The game can be played either *receptively* ("Show me" or "Point to") or it can be played *expressively* ("What do you call this?" or "Why do these belong together?"). If you take turns with the child and each of you has a chance to ask the other for certain cards described by their attributes, or if he plays the game with a group of children, you can observe both the receptive and the expressive levels of his skill. Many children with serious language disorders can play this game skillfully at the receptive level, demonstrating good intact intelligence, yet will not be able to express the concepts on nearly the same developmental level. Children with receptive difficulties who need more time to process language concepts will look quite confused when you ask for more than one attribute at a time. Some will try to repeat the words after you or count off on their fingers, as if to slow down the process; this approach helps them retain the language concept long enough to solve the problem you have presented.

You can also play visual memory games with attribute cards or small toys. Let the child look at an arrangement of cards; then have him hide his eyes while you remove one. Can he tell you in words what is missing? These games, informally presented, do not have standardized age norms. They are nevertheless useful for assessing a child's particular style and strengths.

There are many ways to assess number concepts. "Put six napkins at the table" and "Get two crayons and one piece of paper" employ number concepts and are part of the child's daily routine. Ask a child to count inch-cubes to note whether he has established one-to-one correspondence. If you are in doubt, ask him to put a finger on each block and move it to the side as he counts to make it clear when he has reached his limit. Ask him to give you four blocks and note whether he has to count them out or can easily scoop up the right number. Arrange several piles with a different number of blocks in each and ask him: "Where do you see three blocks? Where do you see five blocks?" Can he tell you right away without touching or counting the blocks? Arrange piles of different sizes and ask him to show you the largest pile, the smallest pile, and so forth. If all these tasks are easy, can he do simple arithmetic problems in his head with no visual referent, such as "If you had two cookies and I gave you two more, how many would you have?" or "If you had six cookies and you ate four, how many would be left?"

Find out about the child's common knowledge: "What day comes after Saturday? When is your birthday? What state do you live in? What are tables made of? Where does milk come from? What kind of work does your mother or father do? Is your brother older than you or younger?"

Interests and Play

So far this guide for observation has stressed a child's skills in using his or her body, perceptual apparatus, and intellect. While these are all crucial to his future success in school and life, there are other areas of concern. How does a child choose to spend his time? What does he choose to think about and work on? Young children develop a style of approaching the world and expressing their interests and changing developmental concerns in play, which establishes them as unique persons. Their play represents the synthesis of their current knowledge, past experiences, present concerns, skills, and concept of self.

The initial question you might ask yourself is whether the child indicates preferences for certain types of activities. Is he an active person or a quiet table-sitter? Can he make choices about what he would like to do? Is he interested in trying something new or does he cling to the familiar? Are his interests broad or narrow, rigid or flexible? If his interests are narrow, do they help to bring him into social contact with other children and with adults, or do they tend to keep him isolated? Are they the sorts of things that will help him to "work" in school? That is, can he sit and concentrate on activities that require some quiet and sustained effort with his hands, eyes, and mind? Can he occupy himself for reasonable periods of time without needing an excessive amount of adult help?

Examine the themes or ideas that characteristically develop in a child's play. He may mention fantasies in regard to his imaginative play with dolls, dress-up clothes, cars, blocks, and other play props. Is there some variation in fantasies? Do the themes or fantasies make sense in relation to the props that stimulated them, or does every different type of material stimulate the same kind of repetitive story? For instance, exciting play about the fire department rescuing people is frequently observed when several children are playing with blocks and trucks. A child who gets excessively engrossed in such a theme so that it pervades his play much of the time is probably communicating a concern. He may need help in understanding something that has happened to him that is still threatening to consider. It would be equally useful to note the themes or ideas that never appear in a child's play, such as parental figures or people who nurture. For example, a child whose father has left the home may never mention him in housekeeping corner dramatic play. Such a child may need help to review their relationship and understand how her life has changed since her father left.

Relationships

The nature of a child's relationships with others also distinguishes him as a person and implies the kind of learner he will be. When you observe a child over time, whether it be for two or three meetings or each day for several months in school, is there evidence that a relationship with individual adults or children grows and builds on previous experience? Hopefully a child can become close, convey feelings, and express concern for another human being. Does he or she choose to spend time with children or adults? Notice what kinds of roles he assumes in relationship to other people. Is he primarily passive, dependent, whiny, bossy, or manipulative with others? Is he flexible in his relationships or does he try to cast every person he works with into an unvarying role relative to himself? What emotional issues predominate in these relationships?

Is he working on problems of trust ("Who will take care of me?"), autonomy ("I want to be boss and do it myself"), or initiative ("Today I'm going to build a castle")? Can this child ask for help with different tasks, accept suggestions, but also take pride in his accomplishments? In short, can you teach him anything? Could he enjoy helping a younger or less proficient child to learn to do something? These relationship qualities pervade everything the child does and determine his capacity to learn. Regardless of the nature or severity of his special needs, his unique personality and style of relating to people will influence the way in which he gets help and compensates for his problems.

Self-Help Skills

To profit from most school situations, children need to take care of their own personal needs and to conform to classroom routines. The degree to which they can function independently in regard to toileting, dressing, eating, resting, changing activities, arriving at school, and going home will depend on age, personal style, maturity, and prior experience with caregivers outside their own nuclear family. The assumption of independence and the ability to ask appropriately for help when needed will give you some insight into emotional as well as physical maturity.

Since young children with special needs are often dependent when they arrive at school, it may help to review the developmental progression toward independence. As in all tasks you must be sensitive to the need for doing *for* and doing *with* before expecting that a child can do *by himself*. Infants still dealing with issues of basic trust expect that their needs will be predictably met. Patterns of eating, sleeping, and eliminating emerge so that caregiving adults learn to anticipate and form routines. Gradually infants give differential clues about what they need, such as food, dry diapers, or stimulation. As mutuality develops, infant and caregiver learn to read each other's cues.

Until a child approaches his third year, the issue of autonomy pervades everything the child does. He or she has achieved enough muscular coordination to handle a spoon and a cup but cannot cut his own meat. He is beginning to be toilet trained, although the adult must take much responsibility for reminding him, taking him, and helping with clothing. He may be able to manage big buttons and pull up a zipper that is started for him. He can take off most of his own clothing but cannot dress himself completely. Although reluctant to let adults assume complete control of when and how transitions will take place, he needs a great deal of help and clear choices about what he can do and when he must terminate an activity. He may even say no when he means yes or when he genuinely needs help.

By the age of four or five, the child becomes independent in most of his personal habits. He can dress himself and is learning to tie shoes. He takes care of bathroom needs without reminders. He handles eating utensils with reasonable skill and enjoys helping out with routines of table setting and cleanup. Because he has some idea about what went before and what comes next, he handles transitions, arrivals, and departures with poise and is able to delay gratification for another day. He may enjoy helping a younger or less proficient child with routine tasks.

Teachers who observe and assess young children in group settings will have many rich opportunities to watch how children handle themselves in these daily routines. While the actual skills the child has acquired are important, so also are the emotional tone and manner he uses in communicating his needs and accepting help. It is useful to comment on the kinds of relationships he establishes in these areas as well as the degree of independence he has achieved.

Getting the Most out of Observations

If you have done a thorough job of observing a child's behavior using the suggested outline, you are ready to draw some conclusions about what you have found. In the preceding guidelines, we have mentioned only a few *age norms*—the ages at which a child ought to achieve some of the skills mentioned. Norms are needed to make decisions about a child's relative strengths or deficits, but they are fallible.

One must consider a child's prior experience very carefully when evaluating findings. A child who has never been exposed to or taught to make geometric shapes will have difficulty producing them when first given paper and pencil and asked to try. What will become significant is his or her improvement when given opportunities to practice. Given coaching and practice, his continued failure becomes more significant than his original difficulty with the task.

Make accurate and careful observations first; then look at age norms. Be aware that no child matures steadily and evenly in all areas of development all of the time. His profile of strengths and weaknesses will make him unique as a learner and will help determine whether or not he needs special help in any particular area. As most children will have some variations in their developmental profiles, it is useful to be able to describe these variations accurately. This is an essential step in being able to decide at what point a learning *style* becomes a learning *disability*.

The duration of learning discrepancies is more important than a child's success or failure at tasks at any given point in time. As a teacher, you can observe children over time in a school or group care setting. With help you can decide when a problem has persisted long enough and whether a specialist ought to be consulted. You can also help a specialist evaluate his findings by suggesting whether or not they are typical of a child's usual performance. To do this you must accurately observe and record the details of a child's behavior over time, comparing them to other children's performance.

Bibliography

Barr, David F., and Carlin, T. Walter. *Auditory Perceptual Disorders*. Springfield, Ill.: Charles C Thomas, 1972.

Bleck, Eugene E., and Nagel, Donald A. *Physically Handicapped Children: A Medical Atlas for Teachers*. New York: Grune and Stratton, 1975.

Bluma, Susan M.; Shearer, Marsha S.; Frohman, Alma H.; and Hilliard, Jean M. *Portage Guide to Early Education*. Portage, Wis.: Cooperative Educational Service Agency 12, 1976.

Caldwell, Bettye M. *The Preschool Inventory*. Princeton, N.J.: Educational Testing Service, 1967.

Dunn, Lloyd M. *The Peabody Picture Vocabulary Test*. Circle Pines, Minn.: American Guidance Service, 1959.

Eisenson, Jon. *Aphasia in Children*. New York: Harper and Row, 1972.

Engel, Mary. *Psychopathology in Childhood*. New York: Harcourt Brace Jovanovich, 1972.

Garfunkel, Frank. "Early Childhood Special Education for Children with Social and Emotional Disturbance." In *Children with Special Needs: Early Development and Education*, edited by Howard K. Spiker, Nicholas J. Anastasiow, and Walter L. Hodges. Minneapolis: Leadership Training Institute/University of Minnesota, 1976.

Gesell, Arnold; Halverson, Henry; Thompson, Helen; Ilg, Frances; Castner, Burton; and Ames, Louise Bates. *The First Five Years of Life*. New York: Harper and Row, 1940.

Granato, Sam, and Krone, Elizabeth. *Day Care 8: Serving Children with Special Needs*. DHEW publication no. (OCD) 73–1063. Washington, D.C., U.S. Department of Health, Education, and Welfare, 1972.

Hedrick, Dona Lea; Prather, Elizabeth M.; and Tobin, Annette R. *Sequenced Inventory of Communication Development*. Seattle: University of Washington Press, 1975.

Jedrysek, Elanora; Klapper, Zelda; Pope, Lillie; and Wortis, Joseph. *Psychoeducational Evaluation of the Preschool Child*. New York: Grune and Stratton, 1972.

Katan, Anny. "The Nursery School as a Diagnostic Help to the Child Guidance Clinic." In *The Psychoanalytic Study of the Child*, vol. 14. New York: International Universities Press, 1959.

Kephart, Newell C. *The Slow Learner in the Classroom*. 2d ed. Columbus, Ohio: Charles E. Merrill, 1971.

Kessler, Jane. *Psychopathology of Childhood*. Englewood Cliffs, N.J.: Prentice-Hall, 1966.

Knobloch, Hilda, and Pasamanick, Benjamin, eds. *Gesell and Amatruda's Developmental Diagnosis*. 3rd ed., rev. and enl. New York: Harper and Row, 1974.

Lerner, Janet W. *Children with Learning Disabilities*. Boston: Houghton Mifflin, 1971.

McCarthy, James J., and McCarthy, Joan F. *Learning Disabilities*. Boston: Allyn and Bacon, 1969.

Mordock, John B. *The Other Children: An Introduction to Exceptionality*. New York: Harper and Row, 1975.

Mowbray, Jean K., and Salisbury, Helen H. *Diagnosing Individual Needs for Early Childhood Education*. Columbus, Ohio: Charles E. Merrill, 1975.

Neubauer, Peter B., and Beller, Emanuel K. "Differential Contributions of the Educator and Clinician in Diagnosis." In *Orthopsychiatry and the School*, edited by Morris Krugman. New York: American Orthopsychiatric Association, 1958.

Rhodes, William C. "The Disturbing Child: A Problem of Ecological Management." *Exceptional Children* 34 (March 1967): 450–55.

Safer, Daniel J., and Allen, Richard P. *Hyperactive Children: Diagnosis and Management*. Baltimore: University Park Press, 1976.

Sands, Rosalind M. "Understanding the Disturbed Preschool Child." *Social Work* 7, no. 1 (January 1962): 88–95.

Shaw, Charles R. *When Your Child Needs Help*. New York: William Morrow, 1972.

U.S. Department of Health, Education, and Welfare. *Responding to Individual Needs in Head Start*. Washington, D.C.: U.S. Department of Health, Education, and Welfare, 1974.

Wyatt, Gertrud L. *Language Learning and Communication Disorders in Children*. New York: Free Press, 1969.

Chapter Four

Making Observations Operational

We shall attempt to illustrate in this chapter the way in which goals stated in operational terms serve to improve the level of competence and skill of preschoolers in dealing with their feelings, their significant others, and their learning materials. Four general objectives that have proven useful to teachers working with young children are as follows:

1. A child can realize his effect on other people and materials.
2. A child has legitimate needs that can be legitimately met.
3. A child can be reflective about his own feelings and behavior.
4. A child can elaborate his ideas and actions when interacting with others or with materials.

These open-ended objectives, developed from questions teachers raised about their work with emotionally disturbed children, reflect a

---

A similar version of this chapter appeared as an article by Samuel J. Braun and Sylvia Woodaman Pollock, "Teaching Disturbed Preschoolers: Making Observations Operational," in *Curriculum is What Happens*, ed. Laura Dittmann (Washington, D.C.: National Association for the Education of Young Children, 1970), pp. 51–61. Revised and reprinted by permission from *Curriculum is What Happens*. Copyright© 1970, National Association for the Education of Young Children, 1834 Connecticut Ave. N.W., Washington, D.C. 20009.

teacher's experiences with children, enhance her ability to organize her observations and plan interventions, and encompass a wide background of theory. In stating each area of learning, we tried to make your chore easier by translating observations of young children into an action plan. Each of the four broad areas of learning suggested provides a structure around which you can chart a course for each child in your classroom.

We found few theories to draw upon that were broad enough and yet still gave sufficient weight to the importance of a child's individuality and resourcefulness. Robert White provides a sufficiently broad position by taking into account the sequence of child development, acknowledging the existence of an inner life, and dealing with the external consequences of behavior. It is from White's notions of competence that much of our language has been borrowed. He speaks of the learning that takes place when an individual actively tries to influence the environment and derives satisfaction from producing effects on both materials and people. Calling attention to times of conflict or crisis, he suggests that defenses may well lead to "*actions* of an efficacious sort which [work] well upon the particular environment and thus [become] the basis for a continuing growth of competence and confidence."[1] His interest is directed toward that aspect of human beings that mediates between self and the environment. Defensive maneuvering is not denied, but it is not the primary focus of attention. This is particularly important to teachers of disturbed children. Their energies are devoted toward engineering the human and material environment so that a modicum of successful negotiations with the environment is insured and a child's sense of competence is subsequently enhanced.

The following case study concerns Alex, a young boy who attended a therapeutic nursery school group at a community mental health center. He met with a teacher, her assistant, and four other children three times a week for about nine months. This case study should not be simply a record of his progress but should demonstrate how you can plan to use all available resources to meet specific goals in each of the four areas of learning we have outlined. Resources are varied: materials, activities, room arrangement, peer relationships, teacher attention, and parent support. You can orchestrate various combinations of these resources, but your success depends on your ability to know when and how to bring various resources to a child.

---

[1]Robert W. White, "Ego and Reality in Psychoanalytic Theory," in *Psychological Issues* 3, no. 3 (New York: International Universities Press, 1963), p. 193.

Your ability to use your self "as an instrument"[2] is the most important resource of all.

Case Presentation

Five-year-old Alex had just been excluded from kindergarten. His family took him to the clinic in September at the urging of Alex's teacher and principal. They reported to the parents that he refused to participate in any group activities and on several occasions was found banging his head on the floor. Alex refused to talk in school except to say, "I want to go 42" (the street number of his house). Although the parents were aware that Alex was reluctant to go to school, they expressed no other concerns. They described how well he played by himself for long periods of time. He repeatedly lined up toy cars, numbers, and letters in rows, to the exclusion of other activities. Both parents boasted about his unusual ability for remembering license plates and serial numbers from cars of family friends.

Alex had one sibling, Virginia, a ten-year-old fifth grader who attended the same school where Alex had been enrolled for six days. She had no difficulties at home or at school. His mother, an attractive woman, was seemingly affectless except for a constant faint smile. Her voice was expressionless. His father, more animated, was preoccupied with his work as a teletype repairman. He often worked long hours, six days a week.

After the intake interview where the family was seen together, Alex was evaluated in a nursery school group diagnostic session. He was a slightly built, dark-haired boy with light, at times almost translucent, skin. Strikingly passive, he needed encouragement to pick up a toy. His speech was echolalic and his ability to relate to people around him was poor. He seemed totally unaware that he could have an effect on the environment. A therapeutic nursery school experience was recommended because of his lack of verbal skills and his limited ability to engage in play activities.

In October, Alex began meeting three mornings a week with four other children: Ray, aged six, a very disturbed, disorganized, unpredictable boy with some verbal skills; Jimmy, aged five, a quiet, but distractable, minimally brain-injured child; Teddy, aged five, a very distractable and seriously brain-injured child with major communication problems, who also had been excluded from public kindergarten;

---

[2]Arthur W. Combs, *The Professional Education of Teachers* (Boston: Allyn and Bacon, 1965), pp. 68–81.

and William, aged five, another kindergarten dropout whose behavior was unmanageable (e.g., kicking the teacher and running on top of the desks).

On the first day of nursery school, each child displayed the behavior for which he had been referred. Those children who had been asked to leave kindergarten were trying to find out how bad they had to be in order to get expelled from this new school—all, that is, except Alex. He was striking because of his obvious inactivity. He draped himself over a wooden train engine two feet long and a foot wide and slowly propelled himself around the edge of the room. He showed no interest in juice or crackers. He gave the teachers the feeling that he had given up wondering about the kind of a response he could elicit from others. There was no evidence of imagination or elaboration in his play.

During the next few weeks Alex kept himself physically separate from the other children, successfully shutting out large segments of the school day. Even when he found himself in the middle of combat between two other children, he did not turn his head or change his expression. When he was not lying over the engine, he hung his body over a chair and played with rubber numbers or letters. He frequently cried for his mother, an act which indicated why he was brought to the clinic in the first place.

Feeling sad and missing someone were legitimate feelings which teachers and other children could support. At school Alex and his teachers could telephone mother at home, draw pictures of her, and talk about what she did while Alex was in school. In addition, Alex's interest in numbers could be transferred to the clock, where he could look to see when he would be going home to his mother; in fact, he learned to tell time in less than a week.

Alex still spent much of his time on the engine, yet there was no reaction from him if another child took it away. His failure to defend this possession best demonstrated his inability to relate to others or to elaborate ideas and activities. The teachers' interest in his behalf gave Alex a new status in the room. Protecting the engine for Alex was a way in which teachers could acknowledge that the need for possessions was a legitimate need that could be met legitimately.

William, clearly the most impulsive and aggressive of all the children; decided one day that Alex might be interesting to tease. He discovered, to his delight, that when he yelled "boo" at Alex, Alex screamed and ran to hide in the bathroom. For Alex it was the first expression of any affect other than sadness. Teachers used the label "scared" for the benefit of both Alex and the other children. They verbalized their observations: his face looked "scared," his voice sounded "scared," and his running away suggested that he was truly "scared." The teachers' objective was to help Alex and his peers learn how to recognize and become more reflective about their feelings and behavior. The intensity of Alex's scream reinforced William's behavior. The two boys soon developed a game in which they experimented with the roles of someone who frightens and someone who is frightened. This was the first evidence that Alex was building an elaborated relationship pattern. He was also learning that it was legitimate for him to feel scared, to show it, and to receive comfort from a teacher.

In mid-November during a routine "nose count," Alex was missing. As the teacher walked by the bathroom door, she heard him talking to himself. He was whispering repeatedly, "Boo, William." Staying with Alex while he practiced in the bathroom, the teacher suggested he move to the full-length mirror in the classroom. There he repeated "Boo, William" with increased volume, while he watched himself at full face and in profile, standing and sitting. Finally he was ready to repay William. William was genuinely surprised, and Alex discovered, to his own delight, that the words had a real effect. He spent the rest of the day running up to William and yelling "boo," carefully watching as William obligingly looked surprised and then laughed. Alex would then retreat to his engine and giggle.

Alex was no longer the passive onlooker. His awakening interest in people and materials only highlighted his inability to recognize himself as a separate entity. When Alex wanted to go home, he usually said, "Mommy wants to go home." He could express his needs but could not yet feel responsible for them. Should another boy hurt his arm and cry, Alex would also appear frightened, holding his own arm in the same area. On occasions when he was eager to go home, he set the hands of the play clock to the hour of departure and suggested that the taxi had arrived. Teachers helped him sort out imaginary from real and distinguish his hurts and wants from someone else's. When they verbally clarified reality to Alex, the teachers were also letting other children know about Alex's concerns (e.g., missing his mother).

But how could Alex feel that he had more of an effect on the world? Teachers helped Alex learn to use words like *yes, no, stop,* and *go* so that he might control the other children when he needed to. If William said, "Alex, give me that engine right now," William knew that teachers would protect the engine for Alex; yet it helped both Alex and William when Alex himself finally said plainly, "No."

At the same time Alex's behavior was changing in school, his parents were noticing changes at home. It was time for the teacher to change the kind of contact she had had with his parents. Previously she had phoned his mother weekly to tell her about what was happening in school, and his mother was only able to listen. But now that she was beginning to have problems managing Alex at home, she had further reason to talk with the teacher. However, when the teacher made a home visit, Virginia spoke for the family. How could the family explain why Alex left public school? The neighbors were asking where he went three mornings a week. Virginia suggested a simple way of describing his difficulty: Alex can't stand up for himself. The teacher. further explained that Alex had begun to tease family members, which was a way of beginning to stand up for himself at home.

In school one day before Christmas vacation, Ray said, "It's eleven o'clock, Alex. Cry for your Mummy." Indeed it was eleven o'clock; Alex wasn't crying, and no one but Ray had noticed. This was one of the positive consequences of making comments to other children about Alex's behavior. As well as making him more interesting and understandable, the comments also helped Alex and the other children become more reflective about themselves and others.

Feeling greatly encouraged by Alex's new composure, the teacher experimented the next day. For the first time, they left school as a group to go for a walk. As they walked to a store that was still in sight of the school, Alex became frightened. Somehow what strength Alex had accumulated could not yet be extended beyond the schoolroom.

After Christmas vacation the group became deeply engrossed in a game about taxis and police officers, stimulated by an event that happened on the way to school. The taxi driver had been stopped by a police officer. (All five children were transported to and from school by taxi, driven by the same person each day.) For days afterward, the popular expression at school was "Hey, pull off the damn road." Alex, again draped over his engine, was involved in the group's transportation game. Unfortunately, the children responded to everyone playing the part of police officer but Alex. He couldn't make his playmates "stop"; he couldn't have an effect.

He did have a chance, however, to make them "go." The children had initiated a game before leaving for home. They ran the length of the long hallway, stopping at the top of the stairs. Since Alex had never enjoyed running, he and a teacher walked ahead to the stairs to watch for the other children. One day the other children waited in the room and listened for the words "ready, set, go," a game initiated by the teacher. On the first try, Alex whispered the words and nothing happened. With encouragement, he finally yelled and was overjoyed to see four children rushing down the hall toward him. He spoke with much more authority than did the police officer who had told the taxi driver to stop. Not only was he feeling that he could affect others, the teachers were helping him to elaborate on a classroom game.

During the last week in January, Alex's mother initiated her first phone call to announce that Alex had beaten up his cousin. The teacher hesitated to respond, expecting her to be upset. However, she said with excitement that this cousin had always beaten up Alex. Finally, Alex had had his revenge. Her only concern was that Alex's father failed to stop him after the cousin had a bloody nose. It was a significant event for all family members.

The next day Alex's face was dirty when he walked through the school doorway. He yelled "hello" and threw his jacket at the teacher. He jumped on the engine, sitting upright, and crashed straight into William. The children were just as surprised as the teachers. A new period of intense provocativeness began, which included kicking walls and tipping over objects. His testing behavior focused primarily on answering the question: "How predictable are the consequences of my actions?" For example, Alex developed an interest in water play. For seemingly no reason, he poured a glass of water on William's head. William warned, "If you do that again, I'll smash you." Alex did, and William kept his promise. Alex seemed to be relieved.

Coupled with his provocativeness was an increased reliance on adults; he would often ask a teacher to help him confront another child about something he wanted. Although he was now able to recognize his wants, he still could not negotiate his needs without help.

During the teacher's next visit with the family, Alex's mother said she knew Alex would need more help now. Although she knew it would be harder to manage him, she insisted she was glad. His father talked with animation about Alex's display of aggression. He confessed that he had always been worried about Alex being a sissy. At that point, the parents talked together about how to set limits for Alex and how to let him know that his own behavior, left unchecked, was frightening to him. Feeling reassured that his parents saw the change as being in the right direction, but also temporary, the teacher supported the parents' theory that Alex's behavior would eventually even itself out.

In school this period of unmodulated aggressive behavior lasted from late January through the middle of March. Much of Alex's aggression was copied from William, the child who had frightened and intrigued Alex most. For Alex the role of the victim had been put aside, and he was now clearly the aggressor. Teachers helped Alex label his behavior as "good" and "bad," assuring him that regardless of how he behaved he was still the same person. They also used the word *new*, encouraging Alex to try out "new" things with the materials in the room that he had previously ignored. He became particularly interested in painting and spent long hours reflectively making representational drawings of "Alex being scared," "Alex scaring William," "Alex helping Teddy," and "Alex getting help from a teacher." He built elaborate climbing structures to try out new motor activity. In addition, the whole group began taking extended walks away from school where they could no longer see the building. Finally Alex's heedless, but frightening aggressive behavior became tempered by his growing reflective judgment. For example, one day in April Alex found himself in the middle of a "traffic jam" with the other children. He ran to his teacher's lap and said, "This is too much traffic for me." To William, who had just taken his engine, he said, "Don't come near me now—you're too mad."

The teacher saw Alex's parents at their home once every few weeks during the spring. Much of their discussion with the teacher focused on their purchase of a new home in a nearby suburb and on Alex's readiness for kindergarten. At the last appointment, they continued to be excited about the move and the changes they noticed in Alex.

Alex had done well in this special group of five children, but would he adapt to a larger group of children? Neither parents nor teachers were certain. His parents confessed that they had been worried, but they supplied the evidence that helped make the decision. They explained that the family had been visiting the beach every weekend. Across the road lived five children, ranging in age from four to ten. The first day there Alex couldn't wait to unpack his suitcase before he ran across the street. His parents watched Alex with apprehension, but they were impressed with how well he handled himself. Teacher and parents concurred that Alex was able to generalize what he had learned in the group.

The family moved in June to a nearby residential town. After helping Alex settle in his new bedroom, his mother had several picnics with him in the playground of the new school located several blocks from their house. She reported that when September came, she accompanied Alex to kindergarten for only two days before he was able to go by himself. In addition, he had found a friend next door.

Alex was ideally placed in an ungraded classroom with fifteen girls and five boys. There he was able to exercise his unusual reading skills; in fact, he went on to distinguish himself by joining the second grade reading group. His parents gained immeasurably by making the final decision about Alex's readiness for school that year.

Discussion

In the previous case presentation, we introduced a young child on the verge of giving up further attempts to negotiate with the world. The teacher, as participant observer, carefully assessed his strengths and vulnerabilities in the context of the developmental expectations we hold for children. At first glance, the teacher might have overlooked the strengths that this child exhibited in the nursery group. He brought with him some ability to use words, the curiosity to look at other people, a persistence to complain about what he wanted, and an interest in symbols (letters and numbers).

These limited abilities were used as building blocks to foster growth. Experiences were presented and fortuitous events were capitalized upon that would ensure success. Each success that Alex experienced increased his sense of competence. The teacher's planning required careful observation, and the successive goals she set demanded a realistic assessment of the possible.

The teacher used a particular resource that is a powerful force in socialization—Alex's peer group. He entered the group as an isolate, having little experience or skills with other children. In order to promote group interaction, the teacher slowly and carefully made him an object of interest to others. She spoke about him to other children. Alex's peers were aware that he had troubling feelings just as they did and that interaction with him frequently brought the attention of the teacher. In addition, some of his own reactions made interaction with him even more attractive.

Some of the steps provided for Alex are worth highlighting, for they represent bench marks in his socialization process. Initially, Alex and the other children arrived in school each having legitimate needs. Alex's wish for his mother was met in legitimate ways: he could call her on the telephone, draw pictures of her, and anticipate going home. That the others were aware of his sadness was suggested by Ray's comments when Alex did not cry. Being involved with William in a scary game also added new dimensions to what he might feel and express. He could be scared and comforted as well as think about scaring others. It is not unusual for young children to behave in extreme ways to portray feeling states. Nonverbal activities often suggest inner states. The feelings involved in clinging or tantrums can find more constructive or understandable expression if they are legitimized. If a child feels confusion, yearns for comfort, or needs to be bossy, he should know that each has its proper time and place in life as well as in the classroom.

Elaboration of activities with materials, such as the clock, or with selected peers was encouraged by teachers. Prior to coming to school Alex had become immersed in materials, but in stereotyped ways. It remained for the teacher to encourage new ways of interacting with materials and people by following a particular interest that Alex showed.

Perhaps one of the more significant gains Alex made concerned his ability to have an effect on his environment. Gradually he learned to use words to change his peers' behavior. If he could simply say no to William while a teacher made sure that William complied with his wishes, he was able to negotiate those wishes. When he said "boo" in such a way that a chain of reciprocal events took place, he had set up a game by expending little effort. By the time he was able to direct the behavior of four boys by saying, "Ready, set, go," he was beginning to savor the fact that he could make a difference. He was eager to practice provocative and teasing behavior even if it meant an occasional clobbering would ensue. This behavior encompassed more than the expression of aggression. He was actively experimenting with a variety of effects that he could have on others, much in the same way that Piaget describes an infant's interest in making a spectacle.

Alex later became more reflective about his behavior and feelings. One of the first steps in this process was learning labels for his feeling states. In this regard, it is not infrequent for young children to be able to learn more about themselves by hearing a person talk about them with someone else. Teachers used this technique with Alex to educate others as well as himself about his behavior patterns. His work with representational drawings showed his attempt to do this for himself. In drawings he could observe himself at a distance in various postures with others and in different moods. Teachers also helped Alex by making his peers sensitive to one another's behavior and feelings. Ray's observation of Alex's shift in behavior pattern at 11:00 A.M. suggests this.

Both children and teachers are involved in socializing behavior and educating themselves about their effects on one another. In a small group, the possibilities for using peers as resources are great. Some of these techniques are also feasible in larger nursery school groups. Focusing on effect, reflectiveness, elaboration, and the legitimization of needs, you can plot a course of action.

This approach to observing and intervening with disturbed young children in a therapeutic classroom suggests building on the strengths a child already possesses. Wisely engineering resources for each child, the teacher plays an important role at home and at school. Close liaison between these two settings is essential. Timing is a critical issue in determining when teacher and family can work together. Active involvement may not be possible until interest and a grasp of the problem have been properly cultivated. With Alex's family contact remained constant but minimal, until a need to solve problems emerged.

We have proposed some aids for translating observations into action after you have collected baseline data on a child. However difficult, you must learn to keep a plan in mind which helps to design activities and also to capitalize on unexpected events in the service of meeting individual needs.

Bibliography

Braun, Samuel J., and Pollock, Sylvia Woodaman. "Teaching Disturbed Preschoolers: Making Observations Operational," In *Curriculum is What Happens*, edited by Laura Dittmann. Washington, D.C.: National Association for the Education of Young Children, 1970.

Combs, Arthur W. *The Professional Education of Teachers*. Boston: Allyn and Bacon, 1965.

White, Robert W. "Ego and Reality in Psychoanalytic Theory." In *Psychological Issues* 3, no. 3. New York: International Universities Press, 1963.

Chapter Five

Family Home Visiting

The teacher-parent home visit is an integral part of any classroom intervention program for young children, especially those with special needs. Home visiting is an obvious convenience for most families with young children. Most parents will prefer you to come to their home instead of arranging an office or classroom conference. Most home visitors have been welcomed with a degree of ease and interest not typically found in an office visit. We have found this to be especially true of low income families.

The home visit has also provided a teacher or other professional with invaluable information about the relationship between the young child and the nurturing environment of his family and surroundings. Complaints about disturbing behavior can become much more understandable in the home context. For example, one social worker was told by parents that their son was hyperactive. After a visit to the family's apartment, his problem behavior took on a different perspective. His spotlessly clean home was decorated with breakable vases and figurines, had no play area, and was close to a busy intersection.

In this chapter, we will first outline some information a home visitor can obtain about variables affecting the behavior of young children. We will then suggest and give case illustrations of some special contributions a visitor can make that can prove helpful to a family. Later we will explore some of the common concerns and issues that beginning home visitors confront.

Assessing Special Needs in a Home Visit

Continuity between the classroom and the home is essential. What is learned about the family may directly influence classroom practice; the language you use, the type and quantity of materials you select, or your arrangement of physical space can be directly affected by what you see and hear in the home. The dwelling itself will give you some idea about what kind of space is available to the child. It may be cramped or extensive, highly organized or unstructured. The things in the home and their arrangement will indicate what is valued.

By listening to how the family communicates with one another, you will form some impression about how the family functions. Accordingly, you will gain some ideas about how they can help you and in what areas you may be of help to them. An important area to assess is the family's use of language with young children. Are words used to convey information, bark orders, punish, or reward? Examine the way a family as a collective unit learns with one another and the home visitor: Do they ask questions and verbally think things through among themselves? Do they use advice? Are they pragmatists who use trial and error? Are they watchful and nonverbal people who learn through imitation or modeling?

As you get to know a family, you will learn how much family members lend emotional support to each other. Do they share chores? Do they criticize or scapegoat one another? Some families are isolated from the community, lacking the resources of extended family, neighbors, church, or other groups. Such information provides you with an ecological sense of the family in the community and some perspective on your relationship to significant others.

To help you as a beginning home visitor to organize the material you will be acquiring and developing, we offer the following outline. It includes suggestions for talking with parents and observing physical surroundings and family interactions in the home. Other important information will come from written material, discussion with people from other agencies, and your own reflections about feelings, attitudes, and hunches after the initial home visit. You may never collect all the suggested data nor should you necessarily try.

Physical Surroundings

1. Describe the general neighborhood, making certain to note the type of residential area, proximity to traffic, convenience to stores and services, and the type of recreation or play space available.

2. Note the characteristics of the population, such as the age range, ethnic characteristics, and the number of other children available for play.
3. Determine how long the family has lived in its present dwelling. It is important to know where else the family lived, why they moved, and how many other moves there have been.
4. Describe the outward appearance and type of the dwelling (e.g., duplex, apartment, project, single-family home).
5. Make a floor plan of the inside to include the physical arrangement of furniture. Indicate where children sleep, where meals are eaten, where children play, and where the television is located, if any.
6. Note the availability of play materials, books, and other resources.

Family Functioning

1. Assess the primary caregiver's style of relating to you, observing the general noise level in the home and striking or typical interaction patterns. Be certain to note the proportion and use of verbal and nonverbal communication.
2. Determine if roles among adults in the home are differentiated concerning budgeting, laundering, cleaning, child care, and other responsibilities.
3. Elicit the primary caregiver's expectations for the child in school, ideas about child rearing and the role of discipline, and concepts about child development.
4. Observe adult-child and peer-child interaction to see how the family communicates needs, expresses feelings, or solves problems.
5. Try to learn how the family copes with crises and whether they abuse alcohol or drugs.

Utilization of Community Resources

1. Find out who the family turns to for help or advice.
2. Learn what role various institutions and social agencies play in the family (e.g., church, social agencies, clubs). Does the family receive financial aid?

3. Get acquainted with the way the family uses medical-dental care. Most families have a pediatrician, a clinic, or a dentist, or they may only seek services on an emergency basis. The financing of medical care often determines whether they use medical care on a regular basis. If medicaid or private insurance is used to pay for service, find out how this is managed by the family. Inquire whether the family has discussed family planning practices with their family doctor.

Individual Child

1. Construct a developmental history listing maturation milestones (ages for sitting, crawling, walking, and language usage) from information supplied by the parents. Include information about the birth and pregnancy, and attempt to assess how the lives of family members were changed by the birth. Comment on the child's temperament or activity level since birth and its similarity to the parents' own style. Ask about what experience a child has had with stressful events (e.g., moving, death, illness).
2. With the parents' or pediatrician's help, specify medical information known about the child: diagnosis for a known "disability," hospitalizations, childhood diseases, allergies (especially to foods), immunizations. Find out from his pediatrician or medical clinic whether he has had vision or hearing screening tests or the Denver Developmental, a common screening instrument for assessing the maturational level of young children.
3. Inquire about previous experiences with separation in day care and play groups, with baby-sitters, and on visits with relatives.
4. Find out about socialization experiences. It is important to know when and how toilet training was accomplished and what words a child uses to let others know he must use the toilet. Learn about eating habits and when self-feeding began. Ask about sleeping habits, bedtime routines, and night fears. Be sure to discover whether a child can dress himself, tie his shoes, or perform other self-help skills. Try to discriminate what he will not or cannot do for himself and find out how he lets others know when he needs help.
5. One of the best ways to learn about a young child is to picture a typical day. Determine from his parents whether the schedule is regular or consistent and what his play activities or assigned chores are. Try to discover when and in what ways parents typically attend to the child.

A young child with special needs is usually referred to an educational program because he has already been identified. It is usually helpful to know when the problem was first recognized or for how long it has existed. What was the precipitating cause or factors associated with the problem or change of behavior? How appropriate is the child's behavior now in relationship to peers of the same age? As important as the questions about delineating special needs are, even more relevant is how and when the family decided to seek help. What prompted them to take steps to enroll in a program? Some families introduce themselves by mentioning that their child has been slow to develop and needs an educational program which they would like to visit and see if they think it will fit his needs. By contrast, another family may express bewilderment about why they came for help. Someone, professional or nonprofessional, may have told them to come because their child "needs help." Because there are truly vast differences among the families who seek help, no assessment of a "special need" or family is complete without gently exploring with a family their motivation for pursuing help.

Contributions You Can Make in a Home Visit

While we have used the term *teacher,* there are other helping persons who work with parents in a home visit or in an educative way. We have emphasized an early childhood education or child development orientation as the basis from which the visitor can make a contribution. We have collected several case studies (which will follow) illustrating some of the skills and understanding that can be conveyed to parents.

The parent also makes important contributions that greatly improve your ability to work with a child. Such a working relationship between you and the parent must be based on the assumption that teachers and parents can help one another. The ability to take each other's advice is directly proportional to your willingness to risk letting each other know what has not worked. Accordingly, you must demonstrate the spirit of cooperation you wish to establish. You may mention what you've noticed at school, what you've tried, which strategies

---

Portions of this section from Samuel J. Braun and Nancy Rodman Reiser, "Teacher-Parent Work in the Home: An Aspect of Child Guidance Services," *Journal of the American Academy of Child Psychiatry* 9, no. 3 (July 1970): 495–514. Reprinted from *Journal of American Academy of Child Psychiatry,* "Teacher-Parent Work in the Home," by Samuel J. Braun and Nancy R. Reiser. By permission of International Universities Press, Inc. Copyright 1970 by International Universities Press, Inc. [Revised.]

failed and those that proved successful. Let the parents know the information you need and the problems that have to be solved. In this atmosphere, you can mutually influence each other's formulation of the problem and proposals for its solution. You can support the parents' efforts sometimes with firmness and sometimes with frequent words of encouragement, but at all times you risk failure together.

There are five areas of learning that are particularly relevant to parents and teachers in a home visit: sharpening observational skills, utilizing a child-development framework, making discreet action plans, anticipating new parental functions, and appreciating the need for encouragement and support of parents. In this section, we have chosen certain examples to illustrate each area.

Observational Skills

Teachers are familiar with the behavior of young children and have developed a set of criteria by which to evaluate a child's growth. Parents do not enjoy the luxury of such objectivity when they observe their children. Frequently they are not sure what to look and listen for—an important focus for parent-teacher work during early visits.

By observing together in the home, you and the parents have a chance to validate each other's observations about a child. The immediacy of the feedback to one another has obvious value; you do not have to rely on a parent's verbal ability or memory. You can focus on sharpening a parent's ability to observe, a skill which is essential to your successful collaboration. If you and the parents together can observe the child and work from the same data, effective plans for promoting growth and new behavior can be made.

****

Scotty's mother referred to her son as "my little Scotty." Indeed, at four years of age he used infantile speech and managed few self-help tasks such as dressing himself or keeping track of his belongings. In school, he frequently responded "I can't" to a variety of simple requests. At home his mother reported the same expectations for Scotty as she did for his 2½-year-old sister. In addition, she asked with doubt if Scotty was learning anything in school. During an early visit, the teacher mentioned several examples of Scotty's emerging new skills and interests. Had she noticed anything that Scotty was learning? His mother said that Scotty had learned the same song from a television program that his younger sister had.

Acting on her observation that his mother expected too little of her son, the teacher asked if she noticed differences between her children. Pointing to her children playing with blocks, she replied, "No, they really do the same kinds of things." The teacher suggested that together they watch the ongoing play that the two children were pursuing on the kitchen floor. After a while the little girl left the blocks, which prompted her mother to note that Scotty seemed able to stay with an activity longer. The teacher then shared her observation that the two year old tried the same way of building about five or six times and seemed to give up when her tower continued to fall. In contrast, when Scotty's tower fell, he tried different ways of balancing the blocks until he had assembled a tower about two feet high. This achieved, he sat back to admire his structure and then proceeded to duplicate the tower with a few embellishments.

The mother looked quite surprised that the teacher "saw so much." The teacher suggested that the mother might have some fun spending a little time each day just watching her children, particularly looking for the differences between them.

One week later, Scotty's mother brought a list of observations, explaining that she had stopped writing after two days because she had noticed too many differences between her children. The teacher commented that since she had such a good collection of differences, they might together look closely at her list and figure out ways to help Scotty learn.

****

Matthew's mother was angry and overwhelmed by her four-year-old son. Mother reported an endless series of undefined, but very real struggles between the two of them. She had tried everything to make him behave. In school, teachers noticed that Matthew did indeed move from one fight to the next. They watched carefully to see what provoked Matthew to be constantly frustrated: he had little expectation of a consistent adult response to his behavior; he experienced no satisfaction when playing with materials or toys; and, above all, he could not let a teacher directly help him.

In the early visits with his mother, the teacher empathized with her distress and asked for details of Matthew's day. She discovered that when the mother went to school each weekday, she deposited her children with various friends and relatives. No consistent arrangement for her children's daytime care was apparent. Sometimes the two children were left together; at other times, they stayed in separate places. At some homes other children were present. Frequently both children were shifted to other places during the day so that even their mother had to go search for them after her return from school. In addition, mealtimes at home were irregular and beds remained unassigned. Life, in short, was confusing.

During the first month at school, Matthew's fighting abated only at times of established, predictable routines, such as hanging up his jacket on his own hook, finding his blue cup, and sitting down for juice. The teacher mentioned this observation to his mother, wondering if she had noticed that Matthew was quick to settle down when he knew what was expected of him and what was to happen next. His mother responded by describing one particularly stressful time of day for Matthew—preparing for the day's child care arrangement.

The teacher suggested that the mother use the same placement for both Matthew and his sister each day for the next two weeks and let Matthew know about this plan. She agreed to try this experiment and carefully observe Matthew's behavior each morning. At the end of the first week she reported that Matthew was indeed fighting less in the morning, but she complained of the effort it took to persuade one sitter to keep her children so many consecutive days. The teacher strongly encouraged her to continue for one more week, trying to make each morning as much the same as the preceding one.

At the end of the second week, the mother reported that Matthew was actually helping her get ready in the morning. The day before she told him to eat breakfast before getting dressed, and he had replied, "No Mamma, first get dressed!"

****

Rather than encouraging Matthew's mother to explore her own attitudes toward control and power struggles, the teacher made an effort to establish a set of routines in the early morning hours to avoid starting each day with a battle. It took mother and teacher one month to clarify a goal and two weeks to implement their ideas. They searched for a limited goal that could be concretely realized and that could be monitored by direct observation.

A Child Developmental Framework

When you are familiar with concepts of child development which attend to facets of cognitive, socio-emotional, and physical development, you will become aware of the maturation and learning process. Accordingly, you will place your data into this framework. Parents' understanding of their child is often influenced by their own childhood experiences, conflicting literature and folklore, and their ability to cope with his uniqueness. Parents can easily become baffled by their child's behavior when they are guided by stereotypes which work against their recognition of individual differences or potentials for growth. The parents' choice of action and their ability to use suggestions are seriously limited if child-rearing decisions are based on such maxims as "My child needs freedom to be creative" or "My child must be taught to be good and obedient."

****

Philip's mother felt herself doubly handicapped as a mother. Philip, the third son, was diagnosed as autistic at two years old. She was well aware of the implications of this diagnosis. As she once elaborated, "If I didn't know so much, I'd be better off; but I do. I've had four years of analysis and my husband is a social worker." She saw Philip's future as bleak; she had read that the odds of recovery are small. She also doubted her ability to be a good mother because she lacked a stable caregiver during her early childhood.

The teacher began working weekly with Philip and his mother together at home. Each visit lasted about 1½–2 hours. During the first visit, the teacher felt as if she were among strangers who lacked familiar patterns of interaction with one another. In the early minutes, Philip banged his hand on the table. When the teacher imitated this gesture, Philip jerked his head around for a glimpse and then banged his hand again. Finally, he offered a fleeting smile as the teacher responded in kind again. During these initial moments, his mother commented on Philip's three common activities: flicking light switches, pressing his body against the washing machine and dryer to feel the vibrations, and lying on soft clothing while sucking his thumb. She exclaimed, "If he'd just talk I'd think there was hope; but I just don't think he'll ever talk, do you?"

The teacher responded by asking the mother to watch. She banged her hand on the table close to Philip and he banged back. To Philip she said, "That's a conversation!" To his mother she said, "I can't reassure you that Philip will talk, but I can continue to visit you at home where together we can try to figure out what Philip will respond to."

The teacher then initiated another game. Using a large cup to cover a smaller cup, she said "hello" and "good-bye" as the small cup was made to disappear and reappear. After establishing a definite rhythm, she then left the small cup covered. Philip grabbed her hand, making it remove the large cup and thus restoring the rhythm. The mother looked amazed, "He's never done anything like that before." The teacher replied, "We've learned something today. Philip responds to sound, imitation, and rhythm, and we can guess that he's willing to take a chance on getting involved in a game."

His mother then questioned if the teacher had been trained to work with children like Philip and if she had had much experience. The teacher answered and added, "Your experience with the two older boys and mine with other children will help us keep track of where we have been and what should come next with Philip. He is our textbook. We have to learn how to help him by watching him and trying different games with him."

****

Brandon's mother was overwhelmed, distraught, and wanted to give up on her "two-year-old monster." She talked about his destructive, demanding behavior and his hatred for his little sister; in fact, she feared that Brandon would kill his little sister if she turned her back for one minute. She switched abruptly to talking about his sweet, angelic face and how he was really still a baby, so soft and cozy to cuddle with. When Brandon fell asleep, she described a few reflective moments when she reassured herself by saying, "Young children are really just animals until they are three—that's when you can civilize them. Oh, if I can only survive another year!"

In a marriage beset by chronic distress, both parents acknowledged that "things have been getting worse since Brandon's birth." A social worker began seeing the parents together, a plan to which they responded with discomfort and relief. This work was crucial for both the parents and for Brandon because they used Brandon as a pawn in their marital discord, barely recognizing him as a separate human being.

The teacher's visits focused on two areas: encouraging the mother to get some relief for herself by leaving her children with a babysitter and gradually helping her to learn something about child development. Brandon's waking behavior consisted of running from object to object, staying with each the five to ten seconds it took his mother to yell no at him. Because "Brandon doesn't know how to play with toys," the parents provided none. The teacher gave examples of how children learn who they are, what they can do, and what's around them by manipulating objects to discover what they can change or modify in their environment. In this family set-up, Brandon could only count on making two things happen: making his mother yell "No, no, Brandon" and making his sister shriek by hitting her.

With his mother, the teacher wondered out loud whether Brandon's driven behavior might be a reaction against his feeling of helplessness, exaggerated by frequent moves and hospitalizations. He could walk, handle objects, and see and hear things happen around him, but he didn't have the skills to control anything. The teacher brought various toys to the home during visits, showing his mother how to present them to Brandon and what he could learn from playing with them. She suggested simple ways to talk to Brandon so that words would be demonstrated as one way of getting things he wanted.

His mother's conceptions of children began to change. She had always been keen to identify them as chronic nuisances. She was beginning to understand that, in many ways, behavior is shaped by the responses to it.

At school Brandon did pick up many simple skills and began talking, using names for many objects and words such as "stop," "no," and "get it." He was able to take these skills home, where he calmed down to a slow gallop.

****

Discreet Action Plans

Training in early childhood education is based on demonstrating complicated concepts through materials and interpersonal relationships. Such an orientation has been cultivated to match the preschooler's style of learning. Verbal explanations tend to elude young children; they explore, question, and explain with their senses. They understand people and things by what they can or cannot do with them. What information they lack they quickly fill with fantasy. Although parents usually appreciate these characteristics in their child, they may lack the ability to make operational what they know. It is here that your ability to demonstrate ideas in action is so effective. The process of "doing" together with the parents and the child becomes the message.

Many families that you will visit live in a most disorganized fashion. For a child, family chaos is often reflected in the lack of personal possessions or places to keep their possessions. Accordingly, such children are liable to run from object to object, passionately claiming something as "mine," only to dump materials on the floor as they are drawn to something bigger and brighter. Not only do objects vanish or break, but the children gain little experience in becoming familiar with play materials.

At first parents do not always appreciate the relationship between learning and playing. They should realize that children need possessions of their own, a guaranteed, well-defined space in which to keep them, and the freedom to explore and experiment with them. You can illustrate this concept by bringing a large carton covered with colorful paper and partially filled with simple, inexpensive materials. Finding a storage space can become a joint project for you and the parent. One mother was inspired by the idea. Instead of storing the clothes of all four children together, she separated the clothing and assigned one drawer to each child. She was pleased to discover that all the children began to take an active role in dressing themselves.

In another family, the mother not only made use of cartons for possession but also began organizing her whole household, initiating some major decorating projects. In a visit after Christmas, she led the teacher into her child's room which, for the first time, was well-organized and neat. She showed the teacher how she had found a second box for him to keep Christmas toys in. With pride she boasted that her son was learning how to be careful with his toys and how to play with them.

****

Genny's family was chronically depressed and disorganized. Their bleak existence was punctuated by external crises, such as being without heat in their apartment in the middle of winter. They temporarily organized their lives around such emergencies.

Both parents complained that their children had trouble playing with each other and with other children. The teacher's notion that the children needed help from their parents in learning to play fell on deaf ears. The suggestion that the parents might even enjoy such play was responded to with both embarrassment and disdain. "What, me build a snowman with Genny and Phil? I'm not a kid!" exploded the father. The teacher searched for ways to unite these parents and children in a single, pleasurable task so the parents could experience fun as adults.

At Christmas time the first such idea proved successful. The teacher brought a large carton of inexpensive art supplies, many of which were common objects found in most homes. The teacher mentioned to the mother the fun that she had as a teacher watching children learn. At the same time she showed the mother how to make several simple Christmas tree ornaments. Although the mother dwelled on her ineptness, she proved quite skillful as she became involved in the task. While they made ornaments together, the teacher casually mentioned other ways children learn. Soon the three older children (ages four to six) joined in. Later, their father sat down after returning from work. They all moved from the kitchen table to the parlor floor where the mother began to teach her children, using many of the words and ideas the teacher had just demonstrated. This scene prompted the father to remark about his wife, "Hey, she's pretty good!" In later visits, the teacher was sometimes able to interest the parents in playing with their children in much the same way they did with the ornaments.

****

When the teacher and Leona's mother tried to talk at home, they were continuously being interrupted by Leona. At school this four year old demanded that every one stop talking and listen to her, even when she couldn't think of anything special to say. In addition, she grabbed any toy that another child was playing with and held on to a given toy long after she moved on to play with something else. The teachers were trying to help Leona learn that there would be enough time and toys for her and that people would listen to her. They played various games that involved waiting and taking turns. As a result, Leona was beginning to be less disruptive in school.

During one home visit, however, Leona was especially provocative. The teacher commented to her mother, in Leona's presence, that she was just beginning to learn about how to wait and that sometimes Leona thought she would never have her turn. The teacher described the various games they played in school that involved waiting. For instance, after they played lotto a few times, Leona knew how long she would have to wait and was assured that her turn would come. The mother was skeptical, so the teacher set up a lotto game for the three of them to play. As in school, she explained how the turns would work. Since Leona was managing the game quite well, the teacher suggested that they could also take turns talking and listening. Each person's talking turn would come simultaneously with the lotto turn.

During the next home visit, the mother related with great enthusiasm how she had told all of her children that they would play the talking-listening game at dinner. Not only did they all try the game, but they discovered that they really were interested in what each person had to say.

****

Three-year-old Christine became panicked when she had to leave her mother. She had difficulty tolerating a nursery school program. Her parents found their whole family life organized around perventing distress in Christine, their middle child. Plans to go to an out-of-town college reunion raised their doubts about how to prepare Christine. The teacher suggested that they start looking for answers in the questions and fears they anticipated Christine would have. After considerable discussion of the trip, they arrived at a series of questions which included: "Will Mommy and Daddy come back?" "Who will put me to bed?" "How long do we have to stay at grandparents' house?" The next task followed naturally.

The teacher helped the parents take one question at a time and suggested several possible ways for them to actively let Christine know they understood and appreciated her fears. For example, each parent would leave a personal article for Christine to keep for them until they returned. Before the parents left the grandparents' house the mother, in Christine's presence, could explain Christine's routines, such as what she liked for a bedtime snack and how much water she liked in the bathtub. To help their daughter understand the passage of time, they could assemble a small book of pictures that depicted such things as breakfast, lunch, dinner, and bedtime. They would leave her crayons and suggest that she put some color on each page after she had finished the activity in the picture. When she reached the last picture would be when "Mommy and Daddy would come home."

The parents implemented these plans prior to going on their first vacation in six years. Christine managed the weekend without panic but refused to speak to her parents on their return until all were back in their own home. There she complained that her parents had left. At the next home visit, her teacher listened and commented on how proud her parents had been that she had managed so well and that they understood she didn't like being away from them. Christine was the first to smile knowingly when the teacher added that after all, liking the separation wasn't really part of the bargain.

****

Anticipation of New Parental Roles

Your presence in the home provides parents with an opportunity to realistically anticipate and plan for the future. For some parents, a child's school entry heralds a new perspective of themselves as having aged and lost important child-rearing functions. Because you are sensitive to these shifts, you can offer concrete suggestions of ways for the parents to bridge the gap between home and school. At the same time, you can help the parents become more aware of the new and different ways in which they are needed by their children during this new developmental stage.

Some parents will react to their young child's school entry by directing complaints at you. Avoiding contacts with the parents or referring them for casework would only serve to intensify their complaints. A mother may have no desire or curiosity to talk about the meaning of her child's leaving her to enter school. In many instances, she is not aware that her angry complaints mirror her feelings of helplessness in sharing what was an exclusive relationship. She may, however, gain a new perspective when given an opportunity to play a new role vis-à-vis the classroom. Assignments, such as helping the teacher acquire materials (i.e., scrap wood, old magazines) or making telephone calls for a future trip, help a mother feel useful. She is able to see that she has not lost her child but has gained a new role in her child's education.

****

Although his mother began to notice more of what Steve was learning at home and at school, she continued to question a tentative diagnosis made 1½ years earlier that Steve was retarded. This clinical opinion had been withdrawn following the discovery and correction of a substantial hearing loss, and the change was confirmed by subsequent psychological testing.

Steve's mother clearly acknowledged that she couldn't bear the thought of her little boy growing up and leaving home. Although the teacher often mentioned that children need their parents for many years, his mother was not comforted by the thought.

In early winter Steve began receiving speech therapy. One part of the treatment was a series of exercises for Steve to do between sessions. The teacher declined his mother's request that this homework be done during school; instead, she encouraged mother to help Steve at home. After procrastinating and debating her ability, his mother agreed to try. Within a few weeks, she all but apologized for having such fun helping her son.

Steve had been placed in a small therapeutic nursery group to learn to play with other children. When the teacher described some of the techniques that were being used in class, the mother responded by inviting a few neighborhood children home to join Steve during lesson time and to remain for play afterwards. When reporting this to the teacher, she said with a tense smile, "You better watch out, I'm going to put you out of a job." The teacher replied that that was exactly her job—to help families so that she would no longer be needed.

By January the teacher suggested that soon Steve would be ready to learn in a larger class, like Head Start. Mother suddenly recoiled, "Oh, no! Not my little Stevey." The teacher detailed his many gains over the previous 4½ months, adding that she would continue to visit her and Steve at home to help with the transition. During the next three visits, his mother tried to think of a legitimate reason why Steve was not ready. The teacher recommended that she visit the Head Start class to see for herself what the children were doing, adding that Steve would need his mother's special encouragement as he moved into a more challenging setting. Finally, on the fourth visit the mother said, "All right, but I better make the call right now while you're here." After phoning to make the arrangement, she turned and sighed, "My little Stevey's not a baby anymore." The teacher stressed again the major growth steps that Steve had made, citing the many ways the mother had helped. His mother amplified, "And I think I've grown as a mother, too."

****

Encouragement and Support of Parents

Through experience in the classroom, you develop deep respect for the unceasing demands that young children make and the care they require. The plight of a parent of a disturbed young child is often lonely and unrewarding. During your visits to the home, offer concrete suggestions and support. This is often the first time that a mother may have experienced the feeling of having shared the responsibilities of child rearing.

In many families these responsibilities are primarily the mother's. Not uncommonly, you may meet only with the mother during the first few months, since the invitation to the father during this time often goes unheeded. By sharing her concerns about her children with you, a mother may realize she can find similar support by calling on her husband or friend.

You may introduce or reinforce this idea by asking on different occasions, "What ideas did you and your husband come up with when you talked together?" The question itself implies an expectation. As a result, mother may begin to seek out her husband to share ideas about understanding and managing their children. When this happens, the father will often join you and the mother. The impetus to meet in this manner may come from the mother, the father, or you. In any case, the decision is always a welcome sign.

Sometimes you can work in such a way that parents learn to use each other as resources. Their support of one another has the potential of becoming far more important than that which you provide. However, mothers and fathers sometimes are unable to attend to their own needs and each other's needs as well as to their children's. If aware of this dilemma, you can often clarify the issues and help parents assign priorities. A possible outgrowth of such discussions can be a referral to another resource for help with their own personal or interpersonal problems.

****

Jamie, the second of three children, was almost six at the time he entered a therapeutic nursery class. His hyperactive and disorganized behavior, unmodified by medication, was confusing and burdensome to himself, his parents, and his teachers. The mother was blamed by her husband for Jamie's behavior, and her in-laws ostracized her for the same reason. During the initial visit, his mother expressed her despair. She didn't know what to do differently. She had told her story to so many different people, but no one had offered any explanation, help, or relief for her or her son.

Over the course of the year, different kinds of help were offered this family. Sporadically the mother saw a social worker at an agency where Jamie was given a variety of medications. One of Jamie's teachers made home visits. In addition, a companion-tutor for Jamie provided some relief for his mother.

The teacher found that any suggestion of plans for managing Jamie at home was futile. His mother was locked in a dilemma, caught between an immensely difficult child and a husband who held her responsible for the boy's symptons, claiming that his job was not the care of his son.

By offering to meet with both parents, the teacher made a delicate attempt to help them help themselves. Agreeing with the father that something needed to be done to modify their son's disruptive behavior, she mentioned that his wife felt the same way, too. Explaining various techniques she had tried, the teacher emphasized that Jamie was also difficult to manage at school. However, she stressed how much the teachers needed to talk with and support each other when nothing seemed to be working. When the teachers needed even more help than they could give each other, they went to other people in the clinic for help. The father, who had listened quietly as the teacher spoke, then asked her to repeat some of her ideas about how to help Jamie.

During the next visit, the mother said that Jamie's father had actually been helpful for a few days, but after a visit to his own mother he had returned to blaming and criticizing her. The teacher suggested that, since the paternal grandmother sometimes cared for Jamie, she be included at the next joint meeting. Although the grandmother came, listened respectfully, and even asked some relevant questions, she persisted in blaming the mother.

The teacher continued to meet with the parents despite the fact that the father sometimes had to leave for work in the middle of the visit. The meetings focused on immediate problems of daily management of Jamie and long-range planning. Throughout these meetings, the teacher empathized with the distress that both parents felt as they considered the possibilities of institutionalizing their only son. Realizing that they were depressed, they were reluctant to share their sorrow with one another. Toward the end of the year, the father and mother went together to visit some possible schools for their son. Although still depressed, they were beginning to share their sadness. During the summer the family took a vacation together and reported that Jamie was considerably calmed. He was even managing in a special class, a far cry from the institution which had seemed a very real possibility a few months earlier.

****

Mackenzie was three years and nine months old when he began nursery clinic classes in September. His parents reported that he was fearful at home, where monsters and imaginary people frequently threatened him. When he was just three, Mackenzie attacked and injured two babies, which prompted his parents' application for help. Pressure for help increased when his mother found herself newly pregnant.

During the first three months of school, the teacher visited his mother at home every two weeks. Although she referred to Mackenzie as "the baby," his mother held unreasonable expectations of mature behavior. She was uncomfortable when the teacher tried to talk about his previous attacks on the babies; in fact, she seldom talked about anything that Mackenzie did. In a valiant effort to sustain conversation, the teacher spent most of the time perfunctorily describing what three and four year olds were like. Even the birth of Mackenzie's sister did not alter the mother's remoteness when discussing him.

Feeling that little progress was being made, the teacher made an evening visit to meet both parents together. Much less guarded and more able to describe specific behavior of his son, the father enabled the mother to talk more freely. They became explicit about Mackenzie's trouble going to sleep and his persistent nightmares. The teacher suggested a bedtime routine for him that included the active involvement of both parents. Previously, he had been allowed to fall asleep while watching television so his mother could avoid a struggle with him.

Toward the end of January, Mackenzie began complaining about one of the taxi drivers who brought him to school. One day he panicked, refusing to go with the driver; consequently, his mother kept him at home. The following week he bit his baby sister's fingers. The teacher reassured the mother that Mackenzie, who had heretofore denied any anger, was struggling with expressing how he felt. They immediately explored the taxi driver issue in the context of his fears, fantasies, and actions. The mother acknowledged that she had always tried to protect Mackenzie from frightening experiences. She now needed the teacher's support to help him face his feelings openly. By inviting early morning telephone contact, the teacher was able to encourage the mother's efforts to help her reluctant son come to school even if it sometimes meant bodily helping him leave home.

By the end of February both parents were more involved in trying to cope with Mackenzie, who was more directly aggressive. The teacher began to visit his dismayed and confused parents every week. She indicated that his increased openness was a good sign. Although he was more provocative, he was feeling that both parents were listening and helping him to control himself.

The parents had begun to tell him bedtime stories as part of a regular bedtime routine. One night as father read "The Three Bears," Mackenzie enumerated the mother bear, father bear, and baby bear but asked where the boy bear was in the story. The parents surmised that he was feeling left out of the family, inasmuch as the parents and baby slept in one room and Mackenzie in another. Having heard what he was saying, they decided to have Mackenzie and the baby share a room. Once more they used each other to talk matters over. When the teacher heard of their deliberation, she let them know how pleased she was that they were acting as a team.

In subsequent visits the parents proved to be increasingly sensitive observers. They continued to use each other to reflect on what they were seeing. The teacher was now utilized to validate the conclusion the parents had already reached after their own dialogue.

****

Common Concerns of Beginning Home Visitors

Beginners are usually haunted by doubts and questions about regular family home visits. Their attention is drawn to unreasonable expectations that they believe parents will have of them and that they hold for themselves. They stand at the threshold imagining that their advice might not work and that they might not be able to answer all of the parents' questions. With suspicions that they will be doing most of the work, they perceive the visit as a time to tell parents what to do even before they know themselves. It is no wonder that beginners feel they will be intruding into a family's life.

Home visiting is, in fact, a matter of mutual consent in which you and the family spend time drawing up a working "contract." If regular home visiting is an expected part of your school's program, your arrival will come as no surprise. However, the agreement you negotiate may take several visits and should be your initial primary concern. Pay attention to developing a trusting relationship; it takes time.

Your contract ought to include when and for how long you will be meeting. Remember to set a time limit. A visit that extends much beyond an hour starts to become wearying and frightening to a family. It also feeds a common fantasy that staying just a few minutes longer will bring some issue to conclusion. For a reluctant parent, brief and frequent visits are easier ways to establish a working relationship.

One of the most common hurdles that you will have to overcome is unexpected interruptions. The television set may be tuned so loud as to make conversation impossible. You may have to ask the parents if they would mind turning the volume down so that you can hear. If appropriate, suggest another time when it may be more convenient for them. The television set, visiting neighbors, or telephone conversations are just some of the ways families have to remind you that your working agreement has not yet been established. Hopefully you will be able to agree on a time and suitable conditions for your meetings.

Another important aspect of the contract you develop is an awareness of the need to attend to the *process* of the work: the need to share information, to try new approaches, to risk failure, and to evaluate your sessions. You are attempting to set a working tone of openness which requires tact, honesty, and the ability to listen and observe without feeling that you must do something. The old adage "look before you leap" seems appropriate before you consider delivering advice. It is more important to establish a climate in which feelings, behavior, and the work itself can be questioned and discussed. Both you and the parents will be identifying the problem you wish to concentrate on. Together you will break the problem down so that you can articulate a series of manageable and feasible goals. In this way, you can more easily experiment with solutions.

No meaningful work can be done without maintaining the climate of *trust* you develop with the family. Your relationship will become solid when you emerge as a reliable and predictable person. Think about the qualities you might want in a person were you in need of help: someone who promises only what can be delivered, someone who is steady if not plodding, someone who accepts you as you are without making judgments, someone who is willing to listen to your feelings, someone who has the patience to work one step at a time, someone who is wise enough to admit a limited knowledge, someone who is sensitive to your racial and ethnic heritage. We might summarize by suggesting that a trusting relationship is established when two parties agree to honor a contract that is specific about where, when, and what help will be rendered.

One feature of your relationship has to do with *confidentiality*. Since you are privy to private information about families, you do not disclose information to others without written permission from parents. Be aware that written records and materials are, in most instances, open to parents. Although agencies and state laws vary in their guidelines, do not encourage parents to read records. However, when records are requested, insist that parents read them with a staff person present so that questions or misunderstandings can be handled. It is helpful to explain in the beginning how records are kept and that they are shared only with those agencies to which the parents have given their permission. Stress with parents your need for continuing frequent communication with others about their child's progress. Some parents are not aware that conferences among fellow workers in different agencies must occur frequently if efforts are to be coordinated. Beware of parents who tell you "secrets." Explore why a confidence is being shared only with you when, in fact, you are not the appropriate person with whom the matter should rest. If you are working on a treatment team, you may be burdened by such information and feel unable to redirect the issue to someone else.

You may find that the most pressing problem confronting a family is not the one with which you can deal. The family may not want you or anyone else to help, or you may not be trained to deal with personal issues (e.g., alcoholism, unpaid bills, marital discord, preoccupation with worries) that are raised. In other instances, the problem that is outlined may not be appropriate to your purpose of helping parents with their children.

Making an appropriate referral to another agency is an art. It takes careful work and time. You need to know how parents feel about the problem and the process of using help and how they perceive the agency to which they are being referred. In the case of a mental health agency, it is wise to know something about the intake procedure. For services such as Alcoholics Anonymous or Alanon (a self-help group for spouses of alcoholics), it's useful to examine your own attitudes about alcohol and to attend one of the sessions; in fact, you may wish to go with the parent initially.

For parents of children with some special needs, they will be well served if you introduce them to other parents whose children have the same handicap. In most communities there are a variety of self-help and/or advocacy groups that provide emotional support, information, and public education. Attendance at local chapter meetings of organizations such as the Association for Children with Learning Disabilities (ACLD), The Association for Retarded Citizens (ARC), The Association for Mentally Ill Children (AMIC), the Epilepsy Society, or the Easter Seal Society gives you an opportunity to introduce yourself and the parents with whom you work to an appropriate resource.

Beginning home visitors also need to find emotional support for themselves. Most find this new role a challenge filled with pitfalls and uncertainties. They value a colleague who can validate their work, bear uncertainty, and offer suggestions. Often such supervision or consultation comes from social workers, psychologists and psychiatrists, or nurses. The role of such colleagues will be discussed more fully in Chapter Eight.

Bibliography

Association for Childhood Education International. *Parenting*. Washington, D.C.: Association for Childhood Education International, 1973.

Braun, Samuel J., and Reiser, Nancy R. "Teacher-Parent Work in the Home: An Aspect of Child Guidance Clinic Services." *Journal of the American Academy of Child Psychiatry* 9, no. 3 (July 1970): 495–514.

Crocker, Eleanor C. "Consultation with Parents." *Young Children* 20, no. 2 (November 1964): 91–99.

Dorenberg, Nanette; Rosen, Bernard; and Walker, Tomannie T. *A Home Training Program for Young Mentally Ill Children*. Brooklyn: League School for Seriously Disturbed Children, n.d.

Fraiberg, Selma. *The Magic Years*. New York: Charles Scribner's Sons, 1959.

Furman, Erna. "Treatment of Under-fives by Way of Parents." In *Psychoanalytic Study of the Child*, vol. 12. New York: International Universities Press, 1957.

Furman, Robert A., and Katan, Anny, eds. *The Therapeutic Nursery School*. New York: International Universities Press, 1969.

Ginott, Haim. *Between Parent and Child*. New York: MacMillan, 1965.

Golick, Margaret. "A Parent's Guide to Learning Problems." *Journal of Learning Disabilities* 1, no. 6 (June 1968): 366–77.

Greenberg, Polly. "Seminars in Parenting Preschoolers." In *Early Childhood Education: It's an Art? It's a Science*, edited by J.D. Andrews, pp. 27–39. Washington, D.C.: National Association for the Education of Young Children, 1976.

Grim, Janet, ed. *Training Parents to Teach*. Chapel Hill, N.C.: TADS, n.d.

Guerney, Bernard G. *Psychotherapeutic Agents: New Roles for Nonprofessionals, Parents and Teachers*. New York: Holt, Rinehart and Winston, 1969.

Hartley, Ruth E., and Goldenson, Robert M. *The Complete Book of Children's Play*. Rev. ed. New York: Thomas Y. Crowell, 1963.

Honig, Alice S. *Parent Involvement in Early Childhood Education*. Washington, D.C.: National Association for the Education of Young Children, 1975.

Jacobs, Lydia. "Methods Used in the Education of Mothers. A Contribution to the Handling and Treatment of Developmental Difficulties in Children Under Five Years of Age." In *Psychoanalytic Study of the Child*, vol. 3/4. New York: International Universities Press, 1949.

Lane, Mary B. *Education for Parenting*. Washington, D.C.: National Association for the Education of Young Children, 1975.

Levine, Rachel A. "Treatment in the Home." *Social Work* 9, no. 1 (January 1964): 19–28.

Minuchin, Salvador. *Families of the Slums*. New York: Basic Books, 1967.

Patterson, Letha. "A Mother of a Retarded Child Suggests . . . Some Pointers for Professionals." *Children* 3, no. 1 (January–February 1956): 13–17.

Sands, Rosalind M. "Family Treatment in Relation to a Disturbed Preschool Child—A Case Presentation." *Journal of Psychiatric Social Work* 23, no. 4 (June 1954): 189–201.

Steinert, Joseph; Atkins, Edith; and Jackson, Theresa. *The Child Entering Nursery School: A Study of Intake Principles and Procedures*. New York: Council Child Development Center, 1953.

Weikart, David P.; Rogers, Linda; Adcock, Carylyn; and McClelland, Donna. "Home Visits." In *The Cognitively Oriented Curriculum*, pp. 79–88. Washington, D.C.: ERIC/National Association for the Education of Young Children, 1971.

Zilbach, Joan J.; Bergel, Ernest; and Gass, Carol. "The Role of the Young Child in Family Therapy." In *Progress in Group and Family Therapy*, edited by C.J. Sager and H.S. Kaplan, pp. 385–99. New York: Brunner/Mazel, 1972.

Chapter Six

Crises Affecting Children's Behavior in School

Drastic change is threatening to all of us. Throughout our lives we invest a great deal in the illusion that we can maintain the integrity of our bodies and our family in a neighborhood of close friends where we work, live, or play. Bodily injury, the loss of significant people, or any major shift in the way our lives are organized are events fraught with confusion and charged emotions. We do our very best to protect ourselves from confronting a reality too painful or too unexpected to bear.

Young children and their families are dealt their share of critical events. Hospitalization, emergency room visits, illness, death of a loved one, divorce and separation, moves—all can be bench marks in development. An appreciation of these life crises often makes understandable sudden changes in a child's classroom behavior. Uncharacteristic sullenness, the loss of ability to choose an activity or to sustain play, or an increase in temper tantrums or aggressive outbursts are some indicators that a change has taken place in a child's life.

Parents or caregivers hold the key. Although they often have information that provides the context for their child's seemingly unexplainable behavior, parents do not routinely mention what is going on to a teacher. Both a family and a young child may be so totally absorbed in a threatening event that they neglect to mention the obvious. Other parents may not recognize that their young child perceives or comprehends sudden changes. We will attempt to sensitize you to some parental dilemmas by suggesting that there are certain universal reactions that make some crises difficult for teachers to handle, too. Their own feelings or past experiences can interfere with their ability to listen or understand.

One of the most universal reactions of a helping person to a crisis is the urge to act or to *do*. In this chapter we will be helping you become more comfortable *not* doing so that you can gain perspective and composure.

Response to Crisis

As helping adults we often forget that there is a time dimension to the process of coping with change. Attempts to cope may take much of a child's intellectual or emotional energy, especially during the first weeks of the crisis. His or her concern may continue over the next year depending on the significance of the crisis or the degree to which fortuitous happenings call the original event to mind.

The first reaction to a painful event is likely to be denial, as if the experience needs to be placed in the deep freeze. It is as if we need some time to disbelieve or to find it isn't so. Such was the case for a three-year-old boy who accidentally fell on a pencil, lodging it in the soft tissues of his cheek and causing one end to extend from one nostril. He was then subjected to X rays, restraint on an examining table, the bright lights of an operating room, and a doctor's probe and tug to disengage the pencil. Later, bandages were applied around the nose and cheek area. He spent the next two days with his eyes tightly closed. His parents had to spoon feed him, take him to the toilet, read to him, and generally cater to his self-imposed condition of blindness. When his teacher came to visit him at home, he still did not dare open his eyes to greet her throughout the visit. As she left, his teacher commented how disappointed his classmates would be when they found out that she had not been able to see him. He could not deny such a compelling invitation any longer. He opened his eyes, prepared to assess the damage.

"Unthawing" is part of that assessment. Lois Murphy describes the experience a boy of three years and three months had when his fingertip was accidently severed in a door slammed without warning by a playmate.[1] The tip was sewn on at the hospital and needed repeated

[1]Lois B. Murphy, *The Widening World of Childhood* (New York: Basic Books, 1962), pp. 115–44.

observations by the doctor. Sam's reactions and comments were recorded in his mother's diary. His "unthawing" included entertaining revenge. When Sam grew old enough, he was going to slam the door on someone younger. He expressed interest in slapping his playmate; in fact, he took great satisfaction in learning she had been spanked. During the first few weeks he cried out in his sleep for his mother. He also resented that his crib had been placed in storage weeks earlier, as though all these events were conspiring to rob him of his wish to be young again.

These continuing expressions of feelings over a four-month period stood in sharp contrast to the first two days of relative silence. During the second day after the accident occurred, his mother wrote of an incident that seemed to "open up the gates": " . . . he was very aggressive and provocative toward me—hitting and punching me repeatedly. Finally I asked him whether he was angry at me because he had gotten hurt, and he said emphatically, 'Yes!'"[2]

"Unthawing" and curiosity go hand in hand. In addition to venting his protest, disappointment, and fear, Sam also wanted to know what happened. He gathered the data by analytic questioning: "Why did she slam the door? Is there blood in the finger? Why does the doctor use black thread? Why does he call it a 'dressing' when he bandages the finger? Did 'Curious George' visit this hospital?" His inquiries were concrete, reflecting his immediate concerns and limited experiences. Until his finger was healed, his cognitive and emotional interests were consumed by these experiences, which represented about four months of his young life.

Along the way he seemed to synthesize his understandings of the accident and its medical treatment by playing out aspects of what had happened. Frequently he assumed the role of a doctor who fixed a toy bear's paws over and over. Sam also prepared penicillin shots for the bear, who could not swallow pills. His play was an important facet of his problem-solving ability—a chance to actively master his concerns and synthesize his knowledge.

Although our examples are drawn from young children's reactions to drastic change, we hope that the similarities between children and adults have not been lost. To be sure, there are some important differences, but adults and children both share an initial need to deny or limit what they can respond to. As their feelings "unthaw," both children and adults may protest and express their anger, confusion, or sadness. In their own ways both assess what happened or what can be done about the problem. While children may work out solutions and possibilities in play, an adult's daydreaming of solutions or holding an

---

[2]Ibid., p. 121.

imagined dialogue is not so different. The similarities are important to emphasize because you can draw upon your own experiences to sharpen your understanding and guide your interventions. Equally important is your appreciation that parents and their children respond to critical events in the same way at the same time but often without parents realizing it.

Young Children's Concerns

The most obvious difference between a child and his caregiver is the fact that children need to be nurtured. When faced with crisis, they often are consumed with an overriding concern about who will take care of them. They naturally fear being abandoned and need physical reassurance and comforting. It is not uncommon to see regressive behavior, such as tantrums, sleep disturbances, and whining, increase in frequency when a child is feeling stressed. They are like calls for help and should be duly recognized as such. Indeed, these regressions are significant; a child usually needs to trust a caregiver before communicating in this way. Whether expressed as tantrums, toilet accidents, or shadowing a caregiver, the need for physical comfort is real. Offering a lap or a hug, combing hair, and washing a child's face are all concrete ways to demonstrate you care. Each of these acts may be especially important to a child, but they may be hard for a parent to provide should both parent and child yearn for caring attention.

Secondly, eager to be in control of some portion of their lives, children are particularly sensitive to feelings of helplessness. They want to feel that they can "boss" or master their destiny. Such thoughts both frighten and comfort them, and their caregivers must often help them strive for moderation. Some children may test limits or regress in an attempt to reassure themselves about what they can control. Setting limits helps! Most teachers learn that a crisis is not the time to make new demands on behavior. Introducing a new curriculum challenge or taking a class trip merely makes more demands on the child, who truly prefers and appreciates those materials he or she has already mastered. Familiar and flexible materials, such as clay, sand, water, or paint, serve to restore confidence and a sense of self-control and provide a soothing retreat. During stressful periods, maintain a stable and familiar routine for the child.

A third difference between adults and children is related to their understanding of the relationship between cause and effect. Because their experiences are so limited, children usually tend to focus the blame or the reason for an event on someone or something within their immediate surroundings. They often gather "evidence" that makes themselves central to causing the event. One moment the parent may be the target for the child's rage; later the child may take the blame. Watching children play often helps clarify for adults how a complicated crisis is being understood and coped with. Some older children may respond to an open-ended invitation to draw a picture or dictate a story; both activities provide an opportunity to express thoughts and feelings.

More characteristically, young children lack the verbal facility to express complex emotions, which makes the task of assessing or understanding their behavior more difficult. A young child is apt to express confusion by appearing aimless and disorganized in the classroom; he or she may not be able to stay with an interest for any length of time. This is especially noticeable if he has not previously behaved in such a way. In this sense he behaves as he feels—as if he were pantomiming the feeling state. Withdrawal and sullenness may effectively portray sadness. His preoccupation may make him oblivious of other children.

As a general rule, if you are in touch with your own feelings when observing, you will be more appreciative of a child's feelings. When you observe no emotional expression or behavioral change in relation to a crisis, you may be secretly relieved; but in fact, you may have more reason to be concerned. Even though it may arouse turbulent feelings in you, it is far easier to help a child who expresses worries in exaggerated separation scenes upon entering or leaving the classroom than one who keeps all of his concerns to himself. During a time of stress, it may be "healthier" for someone to "fall apart" for what seems like no reason at all than to maintain the veneer of good behavior. For an adult or a child, the sign that says "business as usual" during a crisis is a warning.

One last difference between adult and child needs to be raised. Because a critical event is often experienced by adult and child together, the event itself is not the only thing for which a child needs an explanation. Frequently an adult's response—his or her withdrawal, preoccupation, sadness, or irritability—becomes as puzzling as the event itself. In fact, an adult's evasiveness or lack of ease reflects tension, which is communicated to the child.

We have chosen to highlight two common crises: death of a loved one and separation and divorce. Most adults find these events difficult to handle with young children. Because adults are not familiar with their own feelings about death, they are uncomfortable helping young children with this emotionally laden subject. Divorce and separation present another type of problem to the teacher. Dealing with a child whose parents are enveloped in a complex and conflict-ridden situation, teachers are often caught in the emotional confusion of the moment. In either case, learning to recognize and deal with our own uncertainty and feelings are important requisites for helping young children and their families.

Death

Despite the fact that death is evident everywhere, we live in a culture that firmly denies its existence. Such Spartan "socializing" conditions do not help a child mourn a loved one or explore a natural curiosity about death; neither do they adequately prepare teachers or parents to help a child cope with death. Although it is rare for a child to avoid the sight of a dead bird or animal on the street, it is common for an adult to be alarmed when a child comments on what he or she has just seen. If he pokes the carcass with a stick or asks a string of questions, many adults become alarmed that a child shows such a "morbid preoccupation with death."

It is no wonder that when it is time to mourn a loved one or pet, everyone is unprepared. Sometimes adults are so busy at these times that children will be overlooked. Our own unshared feelings and questions need attention before we can listen to the young. We need to sort out our feelings now so that when a death occurs, we are able to answer a child's questions. The subject often requires that we do some "homework."

Children ask concrete questions about death and other natural phenomena. They can understand that a dead person is someone who lacks the properties of life; that is, they cannot sleep, walk, talk, breathe, or eat. Explanations suggesting that death is a deep sleep merely serve to confuse and terrify a young child. He may fear falling asleep at night or may fear that his parents, once asleep, may not wake again. Children are usually interested in learning *when*, rather than *if*, a dead person can come alive again; the younger they are, the more likely they are to believe in such a transformation. In more subtle ways, children wonder if they can join the deceased; they may even worry that the dead person will be jealous that he can't join them or that he will in some way attempt a forced reunion.

Children's ideas about death are often expressed in their solitary or group play where they may "play dead." When adults view such role playing or hear their casual but earnest questions, they can find a child's treatment of death irreverent if not chilling. Yet the ability to intellectually master the concept of death is best done when death is considered a part of everyday life experiences. In the classroom such occasions occur when goldfish die or when passing a dead animal on a walk.

When children are dealing with death, their most immediate concern will most likely be an emotional one, especially if they have had some relationship with the deceased. They may consider such questions as "Who will take care of Frank and me?" or "Could anyone die? Could my mommy die? Could I?" While these questions can be answered with some assurance, others are not so easily dealt with, such as "Why does death happen?" or "Will he go to heaven?" When asked, most teachers tell children that they do not know but that some people believe there is a heaven. Religious beliefs do not usually comfort or reassure children in the same way those beliefs help adults. Exercise care that you do not impose your own beliefs on children. Answer children's questions as directly and honestly as you can, but always take care to listen and to ask questions that elicit their feelings and concerns.

A child's feelings about the death of a loved one may be intimate and difficult to bear for both of you. Anger, sadness, a sense of personal threat, yearning for and a sense of identification with the deceased are strong emotional responses he may not recognize, verbalize, or share without your help. Such feelings are unlikely to be expressed unless you have a trusting relationship and you are comfortable with the concerns he expresses. Neither can a young child broach strong feelings unless he has some assurance that he can and will be cared for and that his parents have given him their approval to bring the subject up. This requires an alliance with parents.

So far we have not indicated who the deceased loved one might be, preferring to emphasize the everyday nature of death and dying as a subject suitable for the classroom. Furman, after studying twenty-three children whose parents died, concludes, "Each surviving member of the family faces so complex and difficult a situation that no form of assistance may seem adequate to the task." She added that many were "fortunate" in their personality makeup and life circumstances so that they could "master the stress and profit from even limited help."[3] She emphasizes how difficult it is to generalize when each of the subjects and their families had such a unique set of experi-

---

[3]Erna Furman, *A Child's Parent Dies* (New Haven: Yale University Press, 1974), p. 296.

ences with the deceased and differing perceptions of the circumstances surrounding the death. However, for young children it proved useful when the surviving parent could help the child understand "the specific circumstances and cause of the parent's death," master the feelings and anxiety related to it, and differentiate themselves from the deceased.[4] Young children needed to "share the family's knowledge of the concrete aspects of death and in their personal and social observances of the death of the loved one."[5] Young children placed heavy demands on their parents and families—an observation worth noting.

Separation and Divorce

Unlike moving to a new house, birth, death, or bodily injury, "separation and divorce" is not an event but a long and complicated series of interrelated events which often has no end. Punctuated by a series of legal steps, each procedure serves as a reminder of loss and provides an opportunity to renew strife. The same painful feelings and unresolved issues are stirred up again and again. Thus, a teacher may feel that the crisis is over when relative peace and equilibrium have been achieved in the classroom, only to discover that an impending court appearance precipitates another period of disorganization, anger, and anxiety. This section on divorce is necessary because in some classrooms, it may be the rule and not the exception that young children are raised in single-parent families.

Most teachers are unfamiliar with divorce laws. Some of these laws are considered to be archaic or moralistic and are now being reformed. Although the laws vary from state to state, a brief outline of the divorce process will help you to understand the process that families will be experiencing. By requesting a temporary restraining and custody order from a court clerk, the mother and father give formal public notice that they have separated. A court hearing is not required unless the mother seeks financial support by petitioning for a

---

[4]Ibid., p. 114.

[5]Ibid., p. 101.

An expanded version of this section appeared in Samuel J. Braun and Dorothy M. Sang, "When Parents Split: A Teacher's Guide," *BAEYC Reports* 17, no. 3 (February/March 1976): 91–97. The same article appeared in amended form in *Day Care and Early Education* 4, no. 2 (November/December 1976): 26–29, 40. Copyright 1976 by Human Sciences Press, Inc., New York, N.Y.

temporary separation and support "court order." Filing an intention of divorce usually comes later. The person who initiates this action is usually required to decide on the grounds for divorce. In some states this decision amounts to making a libelous statement in an adversary proceeding where someone must be judged at fault.

Before a divorce can be settled, a number of decisions must be made: the grounds for divorce, future financial payments, ownership of jointly held property, custody of children, and visitation rights. Alimony usually refers to financial payments from the husband for his wife's support; payments for the care and support of minor children are considered separately. A divorce case is often kept pending or is postponed in court when any of these issues is contested. When a final court order is issued, the customary notion that the mother has been wronged usually guides the decisions in her favor. Because of the number of decisions to be made and the legal context within which they must be made, it is no wonder that the time and anguish spent in reaching a divorce settlement can be considerable.

Preoccupied with their own concerns and confused by the turn their lives are taking, parents may be short-tempered and largely unavailable to their children. The most trivial of requests by a teacher may be overwhelming to the parents. The most innocent questions about a child's daily or weekly routine may precipitate evasiveness or hostility. It is hard to appreciate that for mothers, in particular, the decision to separate often brings additional roles and duties. For example, the roles of parent, cook, shopper, and housekeeper are no longer shared; in fact, additional duties may include budgeting, filling out tax or insurance forms, holding a job outside the home, household repairs, moving, or dating. A teacher who casually suggests to a mother that she spend more time with her young child should do so with caution.

Parents feel overwhelmed in the same way their children do; they are angry that their lives are disrupted, guilty for the part they feel they played, sad for what no longer exists, anxious at the prospect of being alone, and helpless in their inability to control events. It is understandable that parents find it difficult to help children or that children touch on the vulnerabilities of their parents. You may observe with distress as a family suddenly fails in its ability to function. It is difficult to maintain composure when personal feelings such as anger, embarrassment, anxiety, and general discomfort interfere with your ability to talk with parents or children.

A special kind of anxiety is commonly observed in an early childhood program when one of the participating families undergoes the process of separation and divorce. News travels quickly between families and staff, most of whom share their information in private. Neither teachers nor parents can feel immune from the evidence that relationships are fragile, even when sanctioned by law. The personal sense of threat to teachers and other parents in a preschool program and the nature of gossip make separation and divorce a difficult topic to raise in public. This obviously does not make it any easier for teachers who are contending with their own feelings. It is usually helpful for you to find out from separated parents what information the family wishes to share with others. Once again, sharing uncomfortable feelings with a colleague helps you learn how to use or accept your own personal reactions without burdening a child or a family.

Teacher as Helper

We have tried to indicate how teachers can be helpful during times of drastic change. Although they may also feel helpless, they are being helpful when they can listen to parents and children. Listening is not easy because it means learning to listen to yourself as well as others. Although your feelings may sometimes interfere with your ability to listen to others, having feelings is neither unusual nor undesirable. Your ability to share your feelings with a trusted colleague not only lends support and validity to your work, but gives you some indication of how well or in what depth you can handle your feelings with young children or their families. Identifying your own feelings and becoming aware of your own vulnerabilities constitute the first step toward helping children in stress.

Listening also implies willingness to acknowledge and accept the feelings and behaviors of others; asking tactful questions follows. Both are invaluable skills in the relationship between teacher and parents when they have defined expectations for one another.

Both children and parents need physical or concrete support during a time of crisis. For some children a hug or a lap is adequate; others may find a sleeping bag in a quiet area of the classroom a place to find solace. Parents may appreciate being given the name of a baby-sitter or a reliable auto mechanic. Above all, challenges are not needed during stressful times. Both children and parents need familiar activities in a familiar routine.

There are times when behavior precedes the expression of feelings. This is especially true of young children in a crisis, when changes in behavior are often dramatic and noticeable. Helping to verbalize feelings and their relationship to observable behavior in the classroom and events outside the classroom should be undertaken with care and deliberateness. Stick closely to the facts you know to guard against making unwarranted inference. For example, to a child unable to choose play materials or find something to do you might say, "You're having a hard time settling down today. You look upset. Your mom and dad mentioned . . ." Your comment to a child sitting alone in quiet withdrawal might be, "You're all alone over there. You seem sad today. Your mom mentioned . . ." To a child intent on aggressive or disruptive interactions, you might mention, "That's the fifth fight you've been in this morning. Are you angry about . . . ?"

Comments like these suggest that there are reasons for acting in certain ways and that problems can be talked about. They are not meant to be used by adults having no relationship with the child as such an approach would be intrusive of privacy and disrespectful of a child's integrity. Usually teachers are too cautious in bringing up a touchy subject. You can rely on the fact that most children ignore a message that has missed its mark; most take their time responding to an invitation to talk about painful events.

Books about various crises have been written for young children. These stories portray characters who have feelings and are faced with human dilemmas; they help to reinforce the legitimacy of a child's own feelings and their relation to life events. Reading them may help you gather your thoughts. Recommending or lending one to a parent may be much appreciated.

A general rule of thumb is probably in order. Painful reality is not going to disappear and you can not make it "all better" for children. Neither can you answer all the questions. Saying "I don't know" or "It's hard to understand" does not render you ineffective. The tendency to think you must *do* something must be tempered with an appreciation of your limitations. You cannot control events or know every answer. Conversely, a child's capacity to understand cannot always account for the complexity of his situation.

We have tried to suggest that being available to a child or a family does not usually mean action. In most instances, being helpful means being able to bear and trying to clarify the feelings and confusion children and families express when faced with drastic change. In part, this describes the ability to listen, question, and comfort—skills that can be learned. Your capacity to use these skills is usually dependent on what you know, accept, and recognize in yourself.

We also attempted to emphasize that adults' concerns and children's concerns are not dissimilar. While some of the issues that confront children are developmentally based and age specific, in a sense they are also ageless. Thus, you must use yourself as a guide to understanding. When helping people cope with such events, however, it is often wise to find a colleague with whom you can share and validate your own feelings and conduct.

Drastic change should be a part of the "curriculum" for young children even though the subject matter is emotionally laden. It remains an integral part of life and a continuing challenge to all of us.

Bibliography

General

Bowlby, John. "Separation Anxiety." *International Journal of Psychoanalysis* 41, parts 2 and 3 (1960): 89–113.

———. *Separation: Anxiety and Anger—Attachment and Loss.* Vol. 2. New York: Basic Books, 1973.

Caplan, Gerald. *Principles of Preventive Psychiatry.* New York: Basic Books, 1964.

Kliman, Gilbert. *Psychological Emergencies of Childhood.* New York: Grune and Stratton, 1968.

Murphy, Lois B. *The Widening World of Childhood.* New York: Basic Books, 1962.

Murphy, Lois B. and Leeper, Ethel M. *Caring for Children: Preparing for Change.* DHEW publication no. (OCD) 72–17. Washington, D.C.: U.S. Department of Health, Education, and Welfare, 1970.

Parad, Howard J., ed. *Crisis Intervention: Selected Readings.* New York: Family Service Association of America, 1965.

Weiss, Robert S. *Loneliness.* Boston: M.I.T. Press, 1973.

Wolff, Sula. *Children Under Stress.* London: Penguin Press, 1969.

Dealing with Death

Furman, Erna. *A Child's Parent Dies.* New Haven: Yale University Press, 1974.

Galen, Harlene. "A Matter of Life and Death." *Young Children* 27, no. 6 (August 1972): 351–56.

Grollman, Earl A., ed. *Explaining Death to Children.* Boston: Beacon Press, 1967.

Kübler-Ross, Elisabeth. *Death: The Final Stage of Growth.* Englewood Cliffs, N.J.: Prentice-Hall, 1975.

——— . *On Death and Dying*. New York: Macmillan, 1969.

McDonald, Marjorie. "Helping Children to Understand Death: An Experience with Death in a Nursery School." *Journal of Nursery Education* 19, no. 1 (November 1963): 19–25.

Dealing with Divorce

Braun, Samuel J., and Sang, Dorothy M. "When Parents Split: A Teacher's Guide." *BAEYC Reports* 17, no. 3 (February/March 1976): 91–97; *Day Care and Early Education* 4, no. 2 (November/December 1976): 26–29, 40.

Gardner, Richard A. *The Boys and Girls Book About Divorce*. Scranton, Pa.: Haddon Craftsmen, 1970.

Goldstein, Joseph; Freud, Anna; and Solnit, Albert. *Beyond the Best Interest of the Child*. Glencoe, Ill.: Free Press, 1973.

Grollman, Earl A., ed. *Explaining Divorce to Children*. Boston: Beacon Press, 1969.

Stuart, Irving R., and Abt, Lawrence E. *Children of Separation and Divorce*. New York: Grossman Publishers, 1972.

Dealing with Illness and Hospitalization

Debuskey, Matthew, ed. *Chronically Ill Child and His Family*. Springfield, Ill.: Charles C Thomas, 1970.

Freiberg, Karen H. "How Parents React When Their Child Is Hospitalized." *American Journal of Nursing* 72, no. 7 (July 1972): 1270–73.

Haller, J. Alex, et al. *The Hospitalized Child and His Family*. Baltimore: Johns Hopkins Press, 1967.

Hardgrove, Carol B., and Dawson, Rosemary. *Parents and Children in the Hospital: The Family's Role in Pediatrics*. Boston: Little, Brown, 1972.

Lindheim, Roslyn; Glaser, Helen; and Coffin, Christie. *Changing Hospital Environments for Children*. Cambridge: Harvard University Press, 1972.

Petrillo, Madeline, and Sanger, Sirgay. *Emotional Care of Hospitalized Children*. Philadelphia: J. B. Lippincott, 1972.

Plank, Emma. *Working with Children in Hospitals*. Cleveland: Press of Case Western Reserve University, 1962.

Shore, Milton F., ed. *Red Is the Color of Hurting: Planning for Children in Hospital*. Washington, D.C.: National Clearinghouse for Mental Health Information, 1967.

Chapter Seven

Special Needs Children in Regular Classes

Mainstreaming, normalization, integration, heterogeneous grouping, and *deinstitutionalization* are all relatively new words that come from an increased concern for individual rights and reflect the attitude that handicapped children are, after all, *children* first. These words have become slogans used to reverse the previous trend toward establishing special or segregated classes and sometimes entire school buildings for different types of handicapped or special needs children. In fact, in many states you must show cause why any handicapped child should be labeled and separated from his normal peers for educational purposes. Clearly, there is a danger that such concepts can be carried to excess unless we ask some difficult questions: Who are the best candidates for mainstreaming and how will they be selected? How will we properly prepare school personnel to teach in classrooms with such diversity? How will we select curriculum and programming patterns and redesign space for an integrated approach? How will the parents of special needs children fare in such settings?

Some handicapped children had been educated in "normal" classrooms prior to the emphasis on mainstreaming. A few preschools even made a deliberate attempt to recruit one or two special needs children each year. These schools were often affiliated with laboratory or university programs which had ample space, flexible staffing, consultation resources, and an informed group of parents. The children they selected for mainstreaming tended to come from sophisticated, articulate families who were able and eager to pay for private education. Their children usually had a well-diagnosed single handicap and received the best medical care available. A multihandicapped child, a moderately retarded child, or a child with a significant degree of disruptive or distractable behavior was not typically integrated in such a setting. More than likely, an attempt was made to find a bright child with a hearing or vision impairment or a child with an orthopedic difficulty.

Public funding and public policy have forced change. To retain financial support Head Start is required to recruit handicapped children for ten percent of its enrollment. Public schools will receive added federal reimbursement for each handicapped child identified, provided the child's education takes place in the least restrictive environment possible. Consequently, new patterns of programming are emerging: increased availability of special treatment modalities in schools (physical therapy, speech therapy, psychotherapy), more resource rooms, and more partially integrated classes. Teacher education also reflects this trend by emphasizing the "generalist," prepared to work with a variety of children. Indeed, it is no longer possible to become a special education teacher whose expertise is geared toward the "retarded" or some other diagnostic category.

In this chapter, we will point out both the benefits and the problems associated with mainstreaming and offer some suggestions about how to facilitate mainstreaming. Crucial to your success is the ability to help and use volunteers and tutors in your work with special needs children.

What Problems Must Be Solved?

Mainstreaming is hard work. How well you survive pitfalls and challenges depends on your success in coming to terms with yourself. Not all classrooms or all teachers can make the necessary adjustment.

Role Definition in Relation to Children

To many people, *open education* means that each child in your classroom will have a chance to move at his own pace, to select some of his own subjects, and to join you in deciding what teaching and learning styles best suit him. Striking a balance between time spent in industrious "academic" work, time spent broadening interests, and time spent socializing with other children in a well-supervised, but seemingly unstructured environment sounds deceptively simple and is difficult to achieve. Both teachers and children could take the license to brush past each other in a series of fleeting encounters that strain the definition of responsible independence. For some beginning teachers, "open education" becomes an excuse for avoiding a leadership role.

To care for and adequately teach special needs children you will have to be willing to recognize that you are stronger, older, and even wiser than children. Such a statement may seem obvious, but it emphasizes your need to make decisions for and with children. Learn how to use this "power" with sensitivity both to yourself and to the needs of children. Nothing will expose inherent weaknesses in an apparently smoothly functioning classroom group faster than the introduction of one or two difficult special needs children; they may include those who are hyperactive and aggressive, those who are withdrawn and lacking in sensory and communicative skills, or those having difficulty separating fantasy from reality. They challenge you to become active, if not overtly bossy, directive, and intrusive. You will sometimes have to firmly hold children and set limits. At other times, you will need to "test" or evaluate their skills at the risk of exposing their weaknesses and later set out structured or rote tasks to be learned. Still others will need reinforcement measures, which will make you question your right to impose your wishes and values on children. You may even have to motivate children to practice physical therapy exercises that cause pain and produce tears or deprive them of preferred activities to get tutorial or rehabilitative work done.

If you are a neophyte in the teaching field—a new teacher, student, or volunteer—you may have the most difficult time coming to grips with such a role definition. Not yet having accumulated the breadth of experience that gives you confidence, you may be haunted by doubts. You don't have the luxury of referring to a list of other children you have known for whom particular techniques worked. While you are naturally much less certain that your ideas and hunches are worth trying, do not confuse your own uncertainty with philosophical excuses about not wishing to impose your will on a child.

To integrate special needs children and individualize instruction, you must be willing to deprive children of some experiences and insist that they partake of others. In the course of a day you will be called upon to be the benign provider of rich experiences for a large group of children, the confident leader of a small group, or the benevolent dictator who insists that a child complete a lesson based on an understanding or contract the two of you have negotiated about the nature of his problems and needs. You cannot afford to assume the attitude "I'm here if you need me."

Role Definition in Relation to Administration

In some classrooms there may be a place for any given special needs child with mild or moderate difficulties, but *your* classroom may not be such a place. It is not easy to become sufficiently acquainted with your own preferences, teaching style, and strengths and weaknesses to acknowledge that there are some children to whom you cannot be helpful. You may need to find a school and administration willing to honor this realization and actively help you define your own limitations. Some teachers work well with aggressive boys and girls; others do well with shy and passive children. Some feel emotionally comfortable with children who have physical handicaps or disfiguring deformities, while others cannot help such children or establish a climate in which other children can learn to appreciate their struggles and their strengths. Some teach cognitive skills and carry out structured lessons with ease in contrast to those who enjoy working in the personal-social sphere.

When you have defined some of these factors for yourself, consider seriously the kind of school setting and administrative structure that will allow you to exercise those preferences constructively. As a general rule, don't accept a special needs child whom you really don't want in your classroom. However, this rule assumes you have done your "homework" and can state what kind of child you *can* work with. We have already assumed that you need to participate in decision making about placements in your class. Together with supervisors or administrators, you will have to work out the conditions under which you can do an adequate job. Class size, ability to adjust the length of the class day, flexibility of physical space, availability of aides and support personnel, and the existence of resource rooms will enter into your decisions.

In many school systems kindergarten teachers are working double sessions alone with fifty or sixty children each day. Under such circumstances, a teacher will rarely have the energy or capacity to provide for an identified special needs child in her class. In fact, she knows too well that a number of the children she teaches already have unidentified special needs. Unless you can communicate meaningfully to a responsive administration about necessary changes, mainstreaming may do a great disservice to all the children in your class, to yourself, and to the principle of mainstreaming itself.

Role Definition in Relation to Support Personnel

When you enroll a special needs child in your classroom, you can anticipate receiving help from one or more adults. This addition can create tension and challenge your sense of authority in your own classroom unless each adult has a clear understanding of what to expect from the other. You will need to communicate regularly with one another and always keep an open attitude about how you can best work together.

Additional help in the classroom requires you to plan jointly with the adults and communicate your intentions to them about how each detail of the program will be implemented. You can no longer make spontaneous, unilateral decisions or changes of plans without consulting other people. In addition to these complications, you may have to coordinate with a child's tutor or therapist who takes him out of the classroom at specific times for individual work. For example, the weather may be just right for the spring walk you've had in mind. Should children usually meeting with the speech therapist at 9:30 be left behind with an aide? Should you time the walk to fit the therapist's schedule? Decisions like this arise daily when special needs children and their retinue of support personnel are introduced.

You may find yourself assuming more administrative functions, overseeing many factors while spending less time with the children themselves. One lead teacher in a day care class with a different morning and afternoon staff had three special needs children in her group of eighteen. Each child had one or more tutors who, in turn, each had a supervisor. Because it was a laboratory school, the two student teachers and a field work student placed in her class also each had a supervisor. During one week this teacher counted twenty-nine different adults who had become related to her classroom at some time. While this is an extreme example, it did happen. If you find yourself feeling angered, resentful, and out of control of events in your own classroom, it's time to stop and take stock of priorities. *More is not always better*.

When special needs children have tutors, therapists, or resource teachers to work with them as integral parts of a school program, tutors and the teacher may inadvertently compete to determine who is most important in the child's treatment or recovery. Tutors, because they have the luxury of working individually with children and usually receive special supervision for their work, may feel they have a more in-depth understanding of a child's needs than you do. On the other hand, because you spend more time with the child in class, you may feel your relationship is more important and that you are the only one who really understands his needs. Without realizing it, you may devalue the work that goes on in tutoring and see it primarily as a disruption in the child's school day.

Honest, open discussion among team members will help you to appreciate each other's contributions to the welfare of a child. Openly sharing goals, methods, and rationale and honestly soliciting suggestions from others help build a team approach. When you or the tutor are new at the job or unacquainted with each other, such discussions take more time and must be scheduled. Later, when you have developed a working understanding of each other's skills and role, you may informally get together less often. A gesture or facial expression to convey that it's "one of those days," followed by "When can we talk?" indicates that a conference is needed.

To use students, community volunteers, and parents effectively you must become recruiter, supervisor, and advisor. Similar problems will arise in orienting and teaching neophyte tutors. Later in the chapter we will consider their struggles and how you can help.

Role Definition in Relation to Other Agencies

Most special needs children are followed by a medical or specialty clinic that is acquainted with the details of each case. In addition, a child may have a private pediatrician or neighborhood health center that provides routine medical care and helps the parents coordinate the work of the specialists. Sometimes a child needs only a yearly follow-up to be sure things are progressing well. At other times, a child's schedule may include appointments once or twice weekly for various kinds of diagnostic procedures, treatment, and perhaps counseling for the parents as well. When this kind of work occurs outside of school, you may feel cut off and excluded from what is going on. You may wonder about the work outside your classroom and if your daily efforts are appreciated. In a few cases you may find that outside specialists are reluctant to discuss their work with you, considering it confidential or too technical to share. More likely, it is simply a matter of learning to communicate, finding out about each other's role and skills so you have a common basis for discussion.

There can be some very concrete difficulties in communicating with other agencies. You may not have a telephone in your classroom or the coverage to make and receive calls during the school day. Perhaps you must be called between 8:15 and 8:30 A.M. or during your lunch break. Doctors and therapists have similar problems. They can be reached in the ten minutes between appointments, during call hours early in the morning, or at 5:30 P.M. Often the burden of initiating the communication is left up to you, and you may end up wondering if the doctor or specialist is interested. Parents can sometimes be helpful in making the initial contact for you. It takes a while to gather enough confidence about your understanding of a child to feel you can call someone you may never have met and discuss a problem of particular importance to you.

It is useful to establish a method of communicating, such as a monthly telephone time or a system of sending brief observation notes back and forth. This can best be done when the child is first assigned to your class. Don't be content with having such information relayed by a third party, a school nurse, or social worker. As the teacher you need personal contact with others who are working directly with the child. They also need the information you can supply. You may be the only person outside the family who daily spends significant periods of time with the child, and you may also be the first to know about factors in the home that influence the child's capacity to benefit from treatments being prescribed. Take the initiative to establish these contacts. Prepare your observations and questions so you can respect the time constraints on the other person, but remember that what you have to say is worth communicating.

Role Definition in Relation to Parents

Teachers of preschoolers usually have more occasion to communicate with parents than have teachers of elementary school children because they handle many of the same issues with children that parents do. However, in many good preschools the statement "Parents are an integral part of our program" refers to the fact that there are two scheduled parent-teacher conferences a year and that parents are free to visit or contact the teacher at other times. Most parents don't do so. When special needs children are being integrated into your classroom, a new level of parent-teacher collaboration is necessary, and it can be rewarding.

In the beginning, parents will have many uncertainties about enrolling their child in a "normal" class. In some instances their child will be moving from a much more sheltered program where his or her aberrant or immature behavior was understood. In a new environment, they may be anxious for their child to prove himself, or they may feel that their worth as parents is about to be judged. It may also be their first chance to compare their special child with "normal" children on a daily basis. Not only can this be very painful, but they may dread having others see their child's problems or deficits. Fearing the inevitable moment when other parents or children will ask what is wrong, they may be overly sensitive to comments made about their children when no unkindness was intended.

Other parents, having never fully faced the extent of their child's difficulty, may press for mainstreaming as if to deny the extent of his problems. They may unwittingly make unrealistic demands on him and you. When mainstreaming takes place before parents have emotionally come to grips with their dilemma, the parents' adjustment process may actually take longer. Having denied portions of their reality, parents may find it very difficult to collaborate with you.

Another type of problem may arise when parents are unaware that the current placement of their special needs child in a regular class will have to be reconsidered each year. Children who seemed developmentally similar at age three may diverge widely a year or two later, so that the same children no longer belong together. For example, a deaf three year old of normal intelligence may fit well in a preschool classroom where gross motor activities, dramatic play, and exploration of materials are key parts of the curriculum. By age six, however, the normal children are using fluent spoken language to acquire academic skills. In contrast, the deaf child is struggling to articulate a vocabulary of one or two hundred words. Before any new content can be taught, weeks of vocabulary building must take place. Parents may misinterpret the child's initial successful adjustment at age three and react with dismay if he later cannot be "promoted" with his classmates. When accepting the child, you have a responsibility to keep an open dialogue with the parents about what the future holds.

Parents of mainstreamed special needs children, therefore, have some very special needs of their own. Frequent parent-teacher conferences, a regular time for telephone calls, social work services, special topical discussion groups (highlighting hyperactivity and medication or explaining problems to siblings, for example), and support groups where they can meet other parents experiencing the same difficulties are some of the things they need. Parents of preschoolers are not yet "experienced" special needs parents who can be strong advocates for their own children. Initially, most feel bewildered. Be prepared to take on this added responsibility. While guidance personnel in your school can help, *you* are at the front door.

Your new role may be so time-consuming that you find yourself neglecting the "regular" children and their parents, confirming the very fear most often expressed by parents of normal children when their school first considers integrating special needs children. Will the teacher still have time for *my* child and for me? Parents may have other typical fears: Will my child imitate "bad" behavior? Will the academic pace of the class be maintained if some (assumed to be) "slower" children are added? Will there be adequate discipline? Will my child get hurt?

You will find yourself spending more time talking with all parents about your goals and the impact of normal and special children upon each other. You will have to articulate some reasons for your decisions about programming and curriculum and your philosophy about the importance of what you are doing. At first you may feel threatened and caught unprepared by what are really honest requests for information. Teachers have sometimes found it useful to write out their goals for a class and their short-term objectives for each child, posting them publicly for parents and visitors to see. A list of "Simone's new words" or "Nate's physical therapy exercises" removes some of the mystery and helps you to educate all the adults who come and go in your classroom. Chances are you will find some equally appropriate lists and goals for each of the normal children in your room, and parents will all be reassured to discover how much careful thought has gone into planning what looked like "just play." The more open and public you can be, the more parents will be supportive and give you a hand when needed.

Learn to anticipate. Some special needs parents may need your invitation to talk. You can help by voicing some of the questions you think might be on their minds: "Have you found it hard at times when you saw the able children doing things Pete cannot do?"; "Have other parents asked questions about what's wrong with Pete?"; or "Should we take time at a parents' meeting to talk together about it?"

Some teachers have a notebook that goes back and forth with the child each day in which parents and teacher can send brief notes to each other about what has been happening. Through this method, parents can let you know that an important medical appointment is coming up or that toilet training is beginning at home and certain methods are being used. This is where you can mention that to keep pace with the class in next week's project, the child might need some extra time to practice color names or alphabet letters, or you can write out the words to a new song the group is going to learn. Once a pattern for this kind of communication is established, it will take only a few minutes each day to maintain. But you will have to educate parents about what is important by asking questions, such as "Did anything special happen over the weekend? Gil seemed very quiet this morning," or by reporting your observations: "Alice is beginning to look at our faces when we talk. I think it's important to get down on her level and be sure you have her attention before you start to speak, so all your words will seem important."

Role Definition in Relation to Curriculum Planning

In mainstreamed classrooms, curriculum is often more individualized than in regular classrooms. Rarely will you find a series of reading or arithmetic books or a readiness program that fits all your children. You will need a method for assessing the developmental level and tracking the progress of each child. Achievement tests will not help you. Chapter Three of this book suggests ways of assessing each child's skills and needs. You will find some children who use visual skills to compensate for weakness in auditory areas, some who need information translated into sensory-motor channels, and others who need to hear everything verbalized, including their motor movements. If you have accurately identified these different styles, strengths, and weaknesses and assessed each child's developmental level, the next step will be to carefully set individual goals in each developmental and/or curriculum area. Detailed and concrete goals naturally suggest the curriculum.

The concept of *behavioral objectives* has often proven useful to teachers of special needs children. This simply means that you will state what is to be learned, under what conditions it is to be learned, and how you will judge when the job is complete. Instead of global statements like "I want Louisa to learn her colors" or "I want Darren to share with his playmates," you will be able to say "When working with colored inch-cubes in a small group with one adult, Louisa will be able to verbally identify three primary colors when asked, 'What color is this?' " or "When Darren plays in the block corner with several children during free play, he will be able to verbally negotiate with the other children to obtain materials and defend his space." Behavioral objectives such as these limit the area you will work on, allowing you to structure a lesson or play experience so you can measure when the desired behavior has been achieved. For children who learn slowly and cannot extract the clues from the classroom environment, your ability to assess baseline behavior and outline an explicit task will help both you and the child achieve a sense of mastery. Teaching will seem more interesting because small bits of progress will take on new significance.

Teachers unfamiliar with behavioral objectives often recoil when first introduced to them. Such goal statements sound trite, overly simplified, and too "structured." However, most teachers are quite surprised to find how comfortably they can adopt the "lingo" of behavioral objectives and how much it helps to assess and meet individual needs. Goals such as "learning colors" or "sharing with playmates" that seem months or years away become attainable when broken into a sequence of discrete steps.

In a mainstreamed class you will borrow from many different theoretical frameworks as well as from different curriculum programs or series, inventing activities to fit individual needs and making custom-designed games or materials for particular children. Although this sounds time-consuming, most teachers find that when they have assessed behavior accurately and programmed appropriately, they have decreased the time and energy they previously spent in behavior management and discipline. Many management difficulties arise because children are bored or because they are expected to do things for which they have not yet achieved foundation skills. Good assessment leads to goal setting, which naturally suggests what materials and methods will work best with each child. You may be surprised to discover how challenging and rewarding this process can be and how many formerly disruptive and poorly motivated children will become "students."

The bibliography at the end of this chapter includes some references that will help in the assessment/goal-setting/curriculum-planning process. Interestingly enough, some of the most helpful books were written by parents who worked at home with their own special needs children before many special education programs existed. Cameron, Jones and Hart, Kastein and Trace, and Park are especially interesting.

Selecting and Grouping Children for Mainstreaming

We have already mentioned that teachers themselves vary in their readiness to work with certain kinds of children and that the availability of support services greatly influences what is possible. Likewise, children vary in their readiness to be integrated. Some children, maintained in integrated classrooms at great effort, do not really seem to benefit more from being there than they would in a segregated setting more specialized for their needs. Ask yourself: At what point are there *mutual* benefits for the special child and the children with whom he or she will share a classroom? Do the benefits outweigh the problems created?

When children are selected for integration, discussion often focuses on their cognitive or academic readiness to keep pace with the content of the curriculum in a particular class. This may be the easiest part of the problem. With tutoring, small group teaching, and careful collaboration with parents, many children can be given enough special help to master essential skills. What troubles many teachers and concerns most preschool staffs is a child's social adjustment to his new classroom. He can be carefully programmed through a series of supervised structured activities, but what happens during "free play," on the school bus, during outdoor play periods, walking home after school, or when a classmate chooses friends to invite to his birthday party? Many teachers feel social adjustment is the final test, yet they realize that unless a child has a normal peer group with whom to interact he may never achieve readiness and the gap may widen.

In an effort to compensate for developmental lags or immature behavior, special needs children chosen for integration will often be older than the children in the class they enter. Some special needs children with physical problems are smaller than others of their chronological age so that an age difference of two or three years does not stand out. Immature behavior looks appropriate to their size if not to their age. But others are strong and well-built for their chronological age. When grouped with children who are developmentally similar, they tower above the group. If they were normal, such variations might be acceptable; but since they are also aggressive or very shy and withdrawn, they stand out strikingly in relation to the group and seem to call attention to their differences. Many teachers question the value of a plan that seems to accentuate difference rather than strength.

If you participate in decisions about placement of special children in your class, you will want to consider the readiness of the special needs child to undertake at least some of his learning in group situations. If you find that a child is going to need special programming for everything he does and learns, then he is probably not ready. But if periodic individual tutoring or homework done with parents can help him acquire basic skills so he can participate with the group, that is a different matter. For example, either you or the parents can read a story to a communication disordered child ahead of time so he can have a chance to take the words in slowly. You know that when the story is read to the whole group you will not be able to give him sufficient attention and he will lose interest. As another example, you can take an excitable brain-injured child for an advance look at the auditorium where the whole class will be going to view a movie so he can satisfy his curiosity and begin to accept a new routine.

The child's readiness to use or at least understand spoken language will probably be of prime importance, since much of what happens in your classroom involves language. Interest in other children and a curiosity to watch and imitate them are other reasonable prerequisites. A capacity to limit incoming stimulation on his own is also important. If you find yourself changing nearly everything that you do for regular children to keep the situation quiet and unstimulating for the special child, then he is probably in the wrong classroom.

There are no absolute rules for integration. You must look for common denominators that make it possible for the special child to appreciate and enjoy some of what the children in your class are doing. You may feel that certain parts of the day are particularly difficult and select those as times when the child should arrive late, leave early, spend time with a tutor, or use a resource room. Unless you have this flexibility, you may find that instant full-time integration is asking too much of all parties concerned.

Preparing Volunteers for Mainstreamed Classes

Companion tutoring done by volunteers is one method of bridging the gap between what you can do for a special needs child in your classroom and what needs to be done on a more individual basis. Even when children have specialized support services such as language therapy or learning disabilities tutoring, there may be times in the day when you will want extra help to carry a special needs child along with the group, when a child will need very specific individual work on skills he cannot acquire through large group teaching, or when you and the class will need a respite.

Volunteer companion tutors may be parents, high school or college students, members of a neighborhood youth corps, Red Cross volunteers, or others who are interested in learning about special needs, education, or young children. They will find the work challenging and rewarding, and you will find them helpful only to the extent that you help and supervise them when they begin their work.

In training and supervising new tutors, we have observed that they go through three distinct, yet overlapping phases in developing their skills and defining their roles as tutor companions. Outlining these phases may help you know what to anticipate. Because tutors need to talk about the difficulties and uncertainties they confront, the formation of weekly discussion groups of several tutors helps them talk about their experiences and work out future plans with a teacher. Working with these tutors in groups seems to provide mutual support for them and can be a time-saving device for you.

Beginning Phase: Defining and Clarifying a Role

When neophyte tutors are first assigned to work individually with a child, their primary concerns revolve around role definition and establishing a tutorial relationship. They may need a lot of concrete help to select materials, plan and structure a working space, and tell a young child why they are meeting together. Volunteers without prior experience feel awkward in learning to talk to a young child, especially one who may not reciprocate in the conversation. Most tutors also need a chance to discuss the differences between their role and your role as teacher of a group. The tutor soon becomes aware that he or she is in a unique position of establishing a contract with a child to help him confront his learning weaknesses. Like the teacher, the tutor is concerned with simplifying the environment, helping the child focus on one task at a time, and breaking down a task into its component skills to isolate a child's specific deficits.

However, many tutors hesitate to become actively engaged with a child in exploring his problem area. For instance, one tutor was initially unable to confront a child with the fact that she knew he had memorized the words in his book and couldn't really read them. "I can't bear to make him admit he can't do it," she said. Another tutor allowed a child to play for long periods with his Polaroid camera, explaining that there was fine motor coordination involved in her manipulation of the various buttons. He was uncomfortable about approaching her coordination problems directly by placing demands on her for performance on specific school-related tasks. Still another tutor reacted strongly at first when his supervisor suggested that he might ask his child to trace around cardboard shapes. "Tracing" seemed to contradict his previously valued ideas of freedom in the use of creative materials.

In their first few sessions, tutors usually attempt to decipher a child's problems. Even though you may have described them or the tutor may have read a detailed diagnosis, the problems do not become real until the tutor "lives" with the child and assumes responsibility for planning how they will spend time together. In the beginning tutors usually want a large variety of materials in any given session, not yet recognizing the assessment and teaching possibilities that exist in a few simple ones. Ask them to plan beginning sessions in which they are limited to one or two commercial materials such as one-inch colored wooden cubes or paper and magic markers. Such devices may speed up the process of thinking about materials and help them realize the potential of a single item which can be used at various levels of complexity. As described earlier, color cubes are good for spontaneous building, copying a model, reproducing a model from memory, counting, color sorting, color naming, and so forth. Tutors need to be thoroughly familiar with these materials before they can use them creatively and flexibly with children. Encouraging them to handle the materials and use them in role play activities during supervisory times is useful.

The beginning phases of the tutor's role definition might be summarized by the questions: "What am I? What am I here for? How am I doing? How can I arrive at a working contract with this child and my supervisor?" They will need your help to bear the anxiety and uneasiness created by not knowing exactly what to do. They will frequently ask what to do *before* they have observed and gathered some first-hand data. As they begin to trust themselves more, they will be able to see you less as an all-knowing authority and more as a resourceful collaborator.

Middle Phase: Asking Questions to Isolate a Child's Problem

As the tutors become more comfortable with their role, the focus for supervisory discussions changes. Now actively engaged in the task at hand, instead of asking "How am I doing?" they become engrossed in determining the nature of the child's problem and how they can help. Be cautious about supplying too many answers. Tutors need some chance to explore on their own to become inventive teachers. Though you may want them to refer to diagnostic findings from formal tests the children have had, they will hopefully view these results as one of many pieces to a puzzle. They will become aware that their job is one of "asking questions" of the children by presenting activities designed to elicit information about the children's skills, deficits, and learning styles.

For example, the tutor might present a building task using color cubes. If the child could not accomplish it, the tutor would have to revise the task in order to refine the "question." Instead of "Can he build with blocks?" the question might become "Can he use his hands with precision to carry out his ideas?" or "Can he see how the various blocks are related to each other spatially?" The tutor might then be able to devise a series of related tasks to explore these avenues of inquiry and, in the process, learn what foundation skills the child needed in order to be able to build successfully.

Aside from such clear-cut conditions as deafness or cerebral palsy, most children's deficits are not easily isolated; consequently, planning becomes difficult. Tutors need to rely on their knowledge of child development or to consult the literature to make sense out of what they observe. It does not come naturally to a beginning tutor to take several steps backward along a developmental sequence when a child "fails" with a particular material or is simply negative and not motivated. At this stage in the tutors' development, review child development with them.

During this phase, tutors become more comfortable with their roles, with you, and with fellow tutors and begin to use each other more effectively. They have learned to phrase questions so that a colleague can be helpful. It is important to remind them to review how they talk with a child about the nature of his difficulties. Some will have neglected to do this or have said nothing since an initial awkward statement during their first meeting. Some role playing may be in order to check on the tutors' ability to explain the problem in terms simple enough for the child to understand. The tutor might learn to say, "It's hard for you to get your eyes and your hands to work together to do what *you* want them to do. That's why you have such trouble doing puzzles. That will take lots of practice and that's what we're doing together."

During this phase of intense involvement with the children's problems, tutors have developed a tolerance for the ambiguities of the tutorial situation. They are learning what information can be useful and how to get it.

Final Phase: Finding Answers to Questions Posed

In the final phase, most tutors are able to be explicit about the nature of the children's problems and can often develop unique, carefully sequenced plans for each child. In most cases, a working contract with the child has been firmly established. Negativism and disciplinary problems no longer occupy your supervisory time. As one tutor mentioned to her supervisor, "The relationship just isn't a problem any more. Now I need to know ways to work on concepts." The tutor could understand the child's earlier negativism as an expression of his problem, not as a commentary on her tutorial effectiveness.

In this phase, tutors sometimes become frustrated with the available commercial materials and activities they have been using. They begin to focus on curriculum and develop their own unique approaches to the choice of materials. If they have access to a workshop space, they may enjoy designing and making their own equipment out of inexpensive materials. For example, one tutor designed a lotto game in which the symbols to be matched were those letters a particular child had a tendency to reverse or invert. An initial version of the game had only a few symbols on a card. Later, she increased the complexity of the task by adding more letters.

Tutors often find ingenious ways to use themselves and the environment to solve problems. For instance, Betsy needed work in concept development, but she frustrated her tutor by turning every activity into a control struggle. A supervisor helped the tutor focus on the issue of control. He was then able to use a game of "follow the leader" to give Betsy a legitimate chance to be "boss." With Betsy as leader, they played the game for many days on the way to the tutoring room. Betsy used large and small steps, fast and slow steps, and jumping steps. Later, they were able to exchange leadership roles. "You be boss now," Betsy would say. Eventually she could work in the tutoring room with a variety of materials. She could ask for help and could directly approach her specific learning problem areas. The tutor then stopped worrying about whether Betsy liked him as, for the first time, they found a way to work together on Betsy's problems.

In this third phase your supervisory discussions with tutors will focus on specific issues or validate conclusions already reached. Tutors are likely to say, "Here's what's happening . . . What do you think of this idea?" The tutors' energies might also be directed to evaluating their own experiences and their children's progress. Having gained confidence in themselves, they may want to get involved with you in the process of communicating with a child's parents or making plans for a child's future programming.

As tutors look back over their initial experiences, they may need your help to reflect on their own learning. If they have learned a pattern for problem solving, they are ready to approach other children and new situations with considerable confidence.

Why Mainstreaming?

The next generation will include people who will have grown up, gone to school, and worked along with handicapped people. Rather than extol the advantages of sharing our lives with those less fortunate, we can only acknowledge the paucity of such experiences in our own childhood. Few of us can report more than isolated instances where intimate knowledge or meaningful relationships with such persons have existed.

Many people think that early childhood is the best time to begin an acquaintance with special needs persons. Natural, frank, straightforward, and curious, preschoolers approach people without many preconceptions or stereotypes. Fortunately, classroom groupings can be flexibly made because there are few curriculum plans which force decisions about grade levels each year.

As you learn to program properly for children with particular handicaps or learning deficits, other children in the class can benefit. You may be forced to reexamine the way you arrange and use the classroom space as you become more sensitive to the effects of visual and auditory background stimulation, traffic patterns, and the location of work areas. Most likely you will be able to stimulate discussions with the children about contrasts in the way all children behave and learn, fostering an acceptance of individual differences and an appreciation of each child's strengths. You will also become more skilled at analyzing learning styles and identifying strengths or deficits in all children since individualized assessment and teaching become necessities.

Mainstreaming *can* be a positive force. To be successful, however, you must not accept the idea as the perfect remedy. From examining your successes and failures, you can learn and grow.

Bibliography

Barnard, Kathryn E., and Powell, Marcene L. *Teaching the Mentally Retarded: A Family Care Approach.* St. Louis: C. V. Mosby, 1972.

Barry, Hortense. *The Young Aphasic Child: Evaluation and Training.* Washington, D.C.: Alexander Graham Bell Association for the Deaf, 1961.

Bentley, William G. *Learning to Move and Moving to Learn.* New York: Citation Press, 1970.

Bereiter, Carl, and Engelmann, Siegfried. *Teaching Disadvantaged Children in the Preschool.* Englewood Cliffs, N.J.: Prentice-Hall, 1966.

Blank, Marion. *Teaching Learning in the Preschool.* Columbus, Ohio: Charles E. Merrill, 1973.

Cameron, Constance. *A Different Drum.* Englewood Cliffs, N.J.: Prentice-Hall, 1973.

Finnie, Nancie R. *Handling the Young Cerebral Palsied Child at Home.* 2d ed. New York: E. P. Dutton, 1975.

Gordon, Ira J.; Guinagh, Barry; and Jester, R. Emile. *Child Learning Through Child Play: Learning Activities for Two- and Three-Year-Olds.* New York: St. Martin's, 1972.

Granato, Sam, and Krone, Elizabeth. *Day Care 8: Serving Children with Special Needs.* DHEW publication no. (OCD) 73–1063. Washington, D.C.: U.S. Department of Health, Education, and Welfare, 1972.

Hainstock, Elizabeth G. *Teaching Montessori in the Home.* New York: Random House, 1968.

Heisler, Verda. *A Handicapped Child in the Family.* New York: Grune and Stratton, 1972.

Humphrey, James H., and Sullivan, Dorothy D. *Teaching Slow Learners Through Active Games.* Springfield, Ill.: Charles C Thomas, 1970.

Jones, Beverly, and Hart, Jane. *Where's Hannah: A Handbook for Parents and Teachers of Children with Learning Disorders.* New York: Hart Publishing, 1968.

Karnes, Merle B. *Helping Young Children Develop Language Skills: A Book of Activities.* Reston, Va.: Council for Exceptional Children, 1968.

Kastein, Shulamith, and Trace, Barbara. *The Birth of Language: The Case History of a Non-verbal Child*. Springfield, Ill.: Charles C Thomas, 1966.

Kent, Louise R. *Language Acquisition Program for the Retarded and Multiply Impaired*. Champaign, Ill.: Research Press, 1974.

Kibler, Robert; Cegala, Donald J.; Barker, Larry L.; and Miles, David T. *Objectives for Instruction and Evaluation*. Boston: Allyn and Bacon, 1974.

Kozloff, Martin A. *Reaching the Autistic Child: A Parent Training Program*. Champaign, Ill.: Research Press, 1973.

Lagos, Jorge C. *Seizures, Epilepsy and Your Child: A Handbook for Parents, Teachers and Epileptics of All Ages*. New York: Harper and Row, 1974.

Lee, Laura L.; Koenigsknecht, Roy A.; and Mulhern, Susan T. *Interactive Language Development Teaching*. Evanston, Ill.: Northwestern University Press, 1975.

Lehane, Stephen. *Help Your Baby Learn: 100 Piaget-Based Activities for the First Two Years of Life*. Englewood Cliffs, N.J.: Prentice-Hall, 1976.

Meyers, Elizabeth S.; Ball, Helen H.; and Crutchfield, Marjorie. *The Kindergarten Teacher's Handbook*. Los Angeles: Gramercy Press, 1973.

Orem, R. C. *Montessori and the Special Child*. New York: Capricorn Books, 1970.

Painter, Genevieve. *Teach Your Baby*. New York: Simon and Schuster, 1971.

Park, Clara Claiborne. *The Siege: The First Eight Years of an Autistic Child*. Boston: Little, Brown, 1967.

Pitcher, Evelyn Goodenough; Lasher, Miriam G.; Feinburg, Sylvia G.; and Braun, Linda Abrams. *Helping Young Children Learn*. 2d ed. Columbus, Ohio: Charles E. Merrill, 1974.

Robinault, Isabel P. *Functional Aids for the Multiply Handicapped*. New York: Harper and Row, 1973.

Sharp, Evelyn. *Thinking is Child's Play*. New York: Avon Books, 1969.

Smith, David W., and Wilson, Ann Asper. *The Child with Down's Syndrome (Mongolism)*. Philadelphia: W. B. Saunders, 1973.

Taetzsch, Sandra Zeitlin, and Taetzsch, Lyn. *Preschool Games and Activities*. Belmont, Calif.: Fearon, 1974.

U. S. Department of Health, Education, and Welfare. *Responding to Individual Needs in Head Start*. DHEW publication no. (OHD) 75–1075. Washington, D.C.: U.S. Department of Health, Education, and Welfare, 1975.

Warfield, Grace J., ed. *Mainstream Currents: Reprints from Exceptional Children, 1968-1974*. Reston, Va.: Council for Exceptional Children, 1974.

Weikart, David P.; Rogers, Linda; and Adcock, Carolyn. *The Cognitively Oriented Curriculum*. Washington, D.C.: National Association for the Education of Young Children, 1971.

Wynne, Suzan. *Mainstreaming and Early Childhood Education for Handicapped Children: Review and Implications of Research*. Washington, D.C.: Wynne Associates, 1975.

Chapter Eight

Using Supervision and Community Resources

A group of graduate students preparing to be teachers of special needs children were once asked to name the *one* thing they would take with them on a trip alone with a group of preschoolers. One by one, they named their favorite and most reliable classroom materials: trains and wooden train tracks, paints, paper, tinker toys, and play dough. One experienced teacher surprised the group by saying that, instead of materials or games, she would take along a friend to talk with. This wish clarifies the plight of most adults who work for several hours a day with a group of young children. Teaching can be a lonely task. Frustrations and doubts accompany its rewards.

To flourish, a teacher needs to work in a mutually supportive environment where colleagues, assistants, and administrators feel genuine concern for one another. The manner in which a school accommodates this need is vitally important. Most teachers of special needs children learn to use several different kinds of people for help and support: supervisors, consultants, or representatives of other agencies. Whether you turn to one, two, or all three for help depends on the kind of school you work in and your own recognition of what kind of help you can use.

This chapter discusses the process of adults helping each other. Our basic assumption is that to be truly helpful to children, adults also must be able to ask for and receive constructive help from one another.

Since teachers often act as consultants or supervisors to less experienced colleagues while also receiving supervision or consultation themselves, you may read this chapter from more than one vantage point.

The Supervision Process

A supervisor is usually a more experienced member of your profession or discipline and may also be your boss, especially in a small school. Employed by your school to guide and oversee your work, your supervisor is responsible for the quality of your performance and the "success" of the children you teach. Beginning teachers have great difficulty viewing their supervisor as a genuinely helping person and not a critic.

Be aware that the job of supervisor obviously carries with it some occupational hazards. Beginning teachers impose some expectations on their supervisor or boss which may relate more to their prior experiences with authority figures than to present reality. Some assume they will be judged and possibly punished; others anticipate being told exactly what to do at every step of the way. Whether you will feel that a supervisor can help clarify questions and test solutions will probably depend on your own experiences with parents and former teachers.

If you are just beginning to learn about teaching, your supervisor carries a heavy burden of responsibility for your professional growth and for the well-being of the children in your care. Goals for your growth as a teacher sometimes compete with the immediate demands of the classroom situation in which you must perform; a sensitive supervisor usually juggles these different sets of needs.

Being open and reflective about your own perceptions and feelings helps to achieve mutuality between you and your supervisor. The experience of one teacher was revealing. Her teaching supervisor informed her about classroom procedure and family home visiting because she lacked experience working with special needs children. As the year progressed, the supervisor unwittingly felt the teacher's performance on the job reflected her own ability, while the teacher felt she was expected to behave in certain ways. Accordingly, the teacher waited for instructions as each new situation arose. This confusion of responsibility delayed the new teacher's development of a unique teaching style. Having been shielded from making decisions, she did not learn from the consequences of her own actions. Neither the teacher nor the supervisor had trusted the other's knowledge or judgment. Such trust develops over time through honest, tactful communication and familiarity with the skills of the other.

To develop these communication skills, you and your supervisor should meet at regular intervals, weekly or every two weeks. Regular scheduling allows both parties to anticipate needs and develop an agenda for the work to be done. At the beginning of any new supervisory relationship, allow time to get acquainted with each other's prior experience. A supervisor usually asks some questions: "What do you think are your strengths as a teacher?" "What do you think you might need the most help with this year?" "What aspects of yourself as a teacher are you most interested in developing this year?" When supervision is approached in this way, you share the responsibility for making the supervision process a viable one.

As people mature as teachers, some typical problems may arise. Included here are four examples of inexperienced teachers working with supervisors and experiencing typical "growing pains."

Growing Up and Assuming the Role of a Professional

Ann felt like a young girl and acted accordingly. To parents who asked her advice and to supervisors who asked what she wanted help with, she would look puzzled and giggle, "I really don't know." When children in the classroom needed immediate help, she would call for the cooperating teacher. Nonetheless, Ann was well-liked by the children, their parents, fellow teachers, and other program staff. She had the ability to elicit information, feelings, and high performance from those with whom she worked.

From Ann's repeated answers of "I don't know," her supervisor came to understand that she did not see herself as a professional teacher or as an adult who felt responsible for her own actions. Her supervisor attempted to involve Ann in the process of observing herself as well as the families of children in her class, but she could not recall the details of any incident well enough to examine what had happened, nor could she use information when it was offered.

After several months of teaching, Ann exclaimed, "It seems that every time I start something with the children, they are so responsive. Then everything explodes in my face." Her interest in learning to observe had begun. Over the next few months, Ann's observational skills increased dramatically.

Ann began to report vivid sequences of behavior and events, but they were followed by a vague question about what she should do next.

When the supervisor suggested that the answer to her question could be found in the material she had just presented, she became confused. If the supervisor asked what Ann thought was going on or what she would like to see happen next, Ann still replied, "I really don't know." Unfortunately, Ann could not use her own observations to arrive at a formulation of the problem and a plan of action. She was also unable to draw on her own life experience to gain new insight. Ann lacked confidence in her own ability to make conscious decisions and thus passed up most opportunities to initiate a plan of action to help a family. Although she often did sensitive work with parents, she did so in the capacity of a friend who lent support and sympathy.

Ann and her supervising teacher had received psychiatric consultation together. As spring approached, the supervising teacher decided with Ann that she might better profit from the consultation sessions alone. She expressed to Ann that because she would no longer be present during consultation, Ann could decide for herself how she wanted to use the consultation time and assign her own priorities to the topics of discussion.

Ann hesitatingly accepted this plan. After floundering by herself awhile, one day she presented her work with a mother who was facing a serious family crisis. She had learned to recognize the differences between what a friend might do and what a professional helper could do.

Soon after this event, Ann and her husband faced some crucial decisions in their personal life which reinforced Ann's view of herself as an adult. While discussing another family that was undergoing considerable upheaval and stress, the consultant elicited from Ann her own feelings about what she had recently experienced in her own life. Suddenly Ann was able to see the connection, and for the first time she made invaluable use of her own feelings and experiences to understand and help this family. After her next visit with the family, Ann joyfully reported, "Now I see what you mean about using myself to help others." Feeling more grown-up, Ann could now assume the role of a professional with more comfort and ease.

Taking Initiative and Having an Impact

In contrast to Ann, Johanna already felt like an adult. However, she doubted whether she could really have an impact on the children or their parents. One manifestation of Johanna's feeling was that she was consistently late in her responses. Her observations of children and families were excellent; her intuitive and intellectual grasp of their difficulties was sound. But when action was called for, she remained on the sidelines, watching and making motions toward intervention. When she did intervene, she usually did so after the crisis had abated; sometimes a more chaotic situation developed because of her poor timing.

During a supervisory session in midwinter, Johanna mentioned that one of the children in her class was showing signs of acute separation anxiety. The supervisor considered this a "crisis" and wondered what she had been doing to intervene. Johanna replied that she really hadn't done anything except get the facts from the mother. The supervisor emphasized that immediate and specific action was necessary and instructed Johanna to call the mother each morning before school to offer support and direction. Johanna responded to the supervisor's concrete help and implied expectation by offering the same to the parents.

Within two weeks Johanna had dealt with the family crisis. The parents, having experienced her very real and immediate help, became deeply involved in the helping process themselves. Johanna, realizing that she had made a decided and valuable impact on this family, suddenly saw herself in a new light. She spoke with animation and acted as though she expected herself to be an effective agent of change.

Johanna's reluctance to risk failure in helping children and their families was related to her inability to take any action regarding a chronic, serious dilemma that had existed in her own family for several years. Toward the end of spring, she tried for the first time to solve what she sensed to be an insoluble problem. This action represented the change that had occurred in her self concept; she learned she could take initiative.

Learning to Take Yourself Seriously

Gene ignored his own feelings in the classroom as guides to understanding and planning for a child or a family. When he approached one family who experienced every aspect of life as bitterly disappointing, they wondered if they would have to see him. "Couldn't we see someone else?" they asked. Instead of helping them confront this current disappointment, he smiled and said, "Gee, I don't know. I'll have to ask someone." Although he was aware of their disappointment, he did not respond to it.

This example was fairly characteristic of the way Gene approached most tasks or difficult situations. With a shrug of his shoulders, he figured that eventually everything would work out. He held tenaciously to a naïve optimism. If nothing materialized from his work, he showed no concern. He might add, "Besides, maybe it isn't so important anyway."

At school Gene unwittingly antagonized many people. He neglected to return telephone messages, fill out forms, keep appointments, and the like. Despite the efforts of his supervisor to talk about some of these problems, Gene gave the impression that he really didn't care. When he reviewed what he had learned over the year, he was puzzled about two things. He was surprised at himself for being so irresponsible; that was not typical of himself. In addition, he became more aware of his inability to communicate with his assistant in the classroom. In fact, during the year they had expressed some differences of opinion, but each time they left the subject unresolved.

As Gene lingered over these two thoughts, he suddenly became aware of how angry and frustrated he had really felt toward his partner. When his supervisor reminded him that he had not paid attention to his feelings six months ago, he agreed. He suddenly discovered that he had conveniently forgotten important data about himself. Not only had he forgotten to write out forms, clean up the classroom, and perform other duties, but at great expense he had ignored his own feelings. He left his supervisory meeting ecstatic; he had learned to take his "self" seriously.

Sharing Decision Making with Colleagues in the Classroom

Anita and Lenore, who shared responsibility for a group of children with behavior problems, had many difficulties working together. At first, they viewed their very different backgrounds and teaching experiences as justification for their inability to talk to one another. Anita thought she knew nothing about emotionally disturbed children and felt that Lenore, by asking her opinion, was being condescending or was trying to expose Anita's ignorance. Lenore, who consistently felt that people were judging her effectiveness and involvement, thought that Anita's refusal to answer her questions reflected Anita's dislike for her. To her, Anita's actions also indicated a lack of involvement in the total classroom situation, for which Lenore felt some responsibility. In spite of their differences, these two teachers shared a common characteristic. They were both unreflective people who, for different reasons, were unable to look at their own behavior.

Anita and Lenore met each week with their supervising teacher and every third week with the psychiatric consultant. During the early sessions, Lenore asked for opinions about all kinds of details; in contrast, Anita occasionally responded to a question but generally looked alternately preoccupied, annoyed, or disinterested.

After one month everyone involved felt distress. Lenore finally said, "Help! I can't stand this anymore!" The supervising teacher suggested a plan: "Since each of you seems to have such difficulty talking with the other, I'll talk with each of you alone. Then we'll meet together, and maybe I can better help you talk to each other." This two-day plan culminated in a meeting where each teacher, in the presence of the other, repeated to the supervisor what she had said in private. In this way, Anita and Lenore saw that they had misinterpreted each other's behavior. However, each continued to talk more about the other than about herself, albeit with fewer distortions.

By early winter, the supervisor and psychiatric consultant spent much time discussing what they understood had gone on in their respective sessions. In addition, the whole clinic staff discovered that Anita and Lenore would take one classroom incident and discuss it with every staff member in an apparent attempt to reach a consensus about the "perfect plan." Accordingly, the supervision procedure was changed so that Anita and Lenore met with both supervising teacher and psychiatric consultant together every two weeks; in the alternate week, they continued to meet with the supervising teacher alone.

In the first session, Lenore tried to describe a complex situation. The consultant checked with the supervisor about whether they had both understood the same thing. When they discovered they had not, Lenore tried again and invited Anita to help, but Anita could not. The supervisor and consultant then asked each other a series of clarifying questions to check their understanding and tried to validate this with the teachers.

There were variations to this basic approach. Occasionally the supervisor grasped the teachers' idea before the consultant did. Sometimes the consultant could help the supervisor state an idea more concisely and precisely. At other times, one would question the opinion or suggestion of the other or invite critical evaluation of an idea. Although they often agreed on their understanding of a given problem, they usually had very different ideas about how to solve it. At such a juncture, the supervisor and consultant would acknowledge the validity of the other's idea and when appropriate, would find a compromise plan that was mutually acceptable. In short, they demonstrated how a dialogue could be conducted in good humor and in spite of differences.

Gradually the teachers began to join in, initially taking sides with either the consultant or the supervisor. Later they were able to move into a meaningful dialogue with both. By March, Anita and Lenore were beginning to talk to each other more openly with the hint that they could work together. When their attempts failed, the supervisor and consultant could step in to help them get back on the track.

Finally, toward the end of April, Anita and Lenore "clicked." Before each supervision session began, they decided together what they both wanted to discuss. They raised some pertinent issues concerning group process in their classroom, tossed ideas back and forth, and finally settled on a framework in which to understand the problem. The supervisor and consultant were involved as resources for various ideas that might be tried out in the classroom.

At the conclusion of one session, Anita and Lenore spontaneously shared their perception of the year's supervision. They described their feelings of dismay, helplessness, anger, and aloneness during the early months and their mutual thought that supervision was not helpful. Then, during the middle months, they realized that supervision was useful, but they did not understand how. Finally, in the latter months, they were delighted that they were assimilating a process that they understood and could use for themselves.

Responding to primitive or infantile behavior, major life crises, near tragedy, and chronic distress can test your ingenuity and resilience when working with special needs children and their families. In addition to handling the more routine curriculum and behavior management issues, a supervisor is available to help you evaluate and respond to any difficult emotional issues which develop. The regularity of such supervisory meetings is critical. In addition, both you and your supervisor must be willing to examine and evaluate the process of supervision itself. Unless you can become actively engaged in such a dialogue, you are likely to feel frustration, exhaustion, and, more importantly, alienation from the process of teaching/learning.

The Consultation Relationship

Supervisory help comes from someone who has ultimate responsibility for your performance as a teacher. By contrast, a consultant functions without assuming direct responsibility for either patient or program. Consultants take no part in hiring, firing, or promoting personnel, nor do they take medical or clinical responsibility for the students or cases you serve. This is a critical difference which must be clearly understood.

You or your school may decide to employ a consultant in social work, language therapy, psychiatry, or another discipline. This person is hired to help you do *your* job better. Whereas a supervisor might meet and work with children or families to lend support and experience to your work, a consultant normally does not do so. Although a consultant helps you clarify questions, develops hypotheses to test, and makes suggestions, you take those ideas and insights back to your *supervisor* to decide together how and if they can be implemented. This is crucial, because your supervisor is the person who retains ultimate responsibility for the children and families you work with.

If you or your school do use consultation, it is usually best to inform all parents at the beginning of each new school year and the parents of children admitted during the school year: "Dr. Gonzales is our psychiatric consultant. He meets with us regularly to help us understand our work better." Such an announcement can be made by letter, school newsletter, or at a parents' meeting. Provided the consultant is there to help you do *your* job better, that is all that need be said. But before a consultant can spend extensive time with an individual child, parents must be informed and their cooperation sought.

Consultants may work with individual teachers or with a staff group that includes both classroom personnel and supervisors or administrators. If they were to make comments about the adequacy of the performance of given staff members, they would be rendered ineffective and useless as resources. To use their expertise, therefore, you must feel free to ask questions and reveal what you have difficulty with or what you don't know. Since decisions affecting your job security are not based on information shared in consultation, you can trust a consultant with your feelings and doubts.

Consultants differ in the way they approach tasks. Some prefer to observe in your classroom to gain firsthand data about the problems you raise with them. Others rely solely on your ability to describe accurately the behavior or issues that are troublesome. Many consultants prefer to observe at the beginning of a school year to become familiar with the physical setting of the classroom, the general characteristics of the children, and the skills and teaching styles of the staff. After that, they rely on your reporting. The more concretely you can describe behavior, the better help they can be.

The consultant, then, needs to have you do your "homework": accumulate observations, gather background material, note techniques that seem helpful, and thoroughly discuss your information with members of the classroom staff who work together. For instance, most consultants want you to introduce your "problem" child by giving his or her present age in years and months, the family constellation and occupation(s), the type of dwelling and neighborhood in which the family lives, the kind of child care arrangements the family makes, and particular crises or health problems family members have experienced during the child's lifetime. The consultant will also find it helpful if you summarize the child's school experience, prior evaluations, or family experiences in seeking help. Each bit of data can be presented in a sentence or two. Teachers with consultation experience give this information at the beginning of a case discussion without waiting to be asked. Otherwise, a whole session and an intervening week may be spent consolidating crucial bits of material from several different sources. Consultants cannot start to do their part of the job until this information is shared.

Consultants cannot function properly when teachers expect them to faultlessly assess what is wrong or to give detailed directions for solving problems. They are also rendered ineffective when teachers secretly hope they will make absolute judgments about the classroom functioning. Consultants are not there to say whether your work is "good" or "bad."

Neither can consultants read your mind; they will be only as useful as the data you can bring for mutual work. Ideally, the consultant will work with you to form a hypothesis about a classroom management or behavior problem and to help you construct a plan of action and test it out. In this sense, the process is similar to that of supervision.

A critical factor in the consultation relationship is your own realization that you want help. In the following example, a teacher was told to use a consultant who had been assigned by administrative fiat. Teacher and consultant both struggled to find a reason to work together.

****

Mrs. Adams was an older teacher who was prone to complain about all the work she had to do. She told her consultant that she would not *refuse* help, but at the same time she was unwilling to sit down to talk. One day while the consultant was visiting elsewhere in the building, she received an urgent message to go to Mrs. Adams' classroom. She found Mrs. Adams in the hall, holding onto a struggling, panicked child named Mark who was crying that he wanted to go home. Mrs. Adams explained that he had just run home following a reprimand from an aide. Brought back under duress, Mark had become increasingly upset. As Mrs. Adams explained that she was adamant that Mark remain, he suddenly excaped from her arm. He was caught and held by the consultant, to whom he sobbed, "I'm going to scare the wits out of you." The consultant decided to take this opportunity to work with Mark in front of Mrs. Adams. Because it was the first time Mrs. Adams had actually asked for help, the consultant decided to acquaint Mrs. Adams with her skills, even though she risked being considered as just another pair of hands for the teacher.

Mrs. Adams listened to the dialogue between Mark and the consultant as she went back to her classroom work. Periodically, she returned to their vicinity. The consultant told Mark that she could tell he was a strong boy. Was he strong enough to run very fast? "Yes," he blubbered. Was he strong enough to climb high? "Yes," he said amidst sniffles. "I can climb a tree." Was his voice strong enough to yell as loud as he wanted to? "Yes," he shouted and stopped struggling. Were his legs strong enough to jump on the stairs? "Yes," he said. Would he show her how he jumped? Mark proceeded to jump down three steps. When she commented on his strength, he began to smile.

Because Mrs. Adams did not know that "he could jump so well with his strong legs," the consultant and Mark called for her to watch. Mrs. Adams smiled and said, "Good boy, Mark" and continued to another part of the room. The consultant suggested that they could tell one of Mark's friends how strong he was. Mark extended his hand to her as they went off to find Bernie. After they had found Bernie, the consultant told Mark she had to leave and suggested that he and Bernie could use their strong arms to build a big building with blocks. She added that the reprimanding aide might like to see them work together. Mark and Bernie headed toward the block corner and called for the aide, who joined them there.

After class was over, the consultant debated whether to approach Mrs. Adams and decided to wait and see if she wanted to talk. A few minutes later, Mrs. Adams came into the classroom, asking, "Do you have some time for me today?" She beckoned the consultant to a distant table and proceeded to ask, "What is your magic?" The consultant explained that she had helped Mark to get more in touch with the active part of himself. Mrs. Adams seemed to be listening and commented, "Well, I knew if the two of us got together, one of us would be able to do something." She went on to describe some events that morning which she thought she had handled well. The consultant offered some elaborations on why Mrs. Adams' actions were particularly helpful to certain children. This was the first time the two had been able to carry on a conversation sitting down. The consultant had become accustomed to hearing a barrage of complaints as the teacher was rushing off to another task.

****

If your school expects you to make use of consultants that it already employs, take the opportunity to discuss the consultation process itself with your consultant at the beginning of the school year. Find out how he or she is accustomed to proceeding and what is expected of you in preparation for each session. Establish a time during consultation when you can critique your sessions, mentioning what was helpful, what was unclear, and so forth.

If you have the opportunity to choose a consultant, think first about the kind of help you need. Do you need more expertise in your own discipline, specialized help in an allied area that you know little about, or advice about families? Will you be asking for occasional help with difficult cases or regularly scheduled meetings to evaluate how things are going? You may already know someone you have found helpful in the past. If not, call your local mental health center, family service agency, hospital child development clinic, or elementary school guidance department. Ask if they provide consultation for neighboring early childhood centers and describe the kind of help you are looking for. If a person is available and interested, arrange a visit at your school for a chance to talk and decide whether you both feel you can establish a working relationship based on some common interests and beliefs. A good relationship between you and your consultant requires mutual respect and the ability to establish some common goals. Allow yourselves a chance to get acquainted and then draw up an informal consultation agreement. This may be a verbal agreement or an exchange of letters. The process of deciding *together* is what matters.

Some school budgets have provisions for paying consultants. If not, you may decide to pay someone yourself. (Always make such an arrangement with the knowledge and encouragement of your supervisor or boss.) Some free-lance consultants have a set fee that they charge for an hour or a session. Sometimes consultation is one of the free community services provided to early childhood facilities by a local mental health center or school system. There may be a kind of "barter" arrangement where, in return for providing consultation, an agency is occasionally able to place a patient or client in your school, or consulting at your school may be a training experience for young mental health professionals learning about children and/or consultation. Be sure that the question of fees or exchange of services is discussed and understood by both parties in the consultation agreement and, where appropriate, by the administrators of both places as well.

Collaboration with Other Agencies

Many special needs children have already been diagnosed at a clinic or hospital when assigned to your class. They may continue to receive outside treatment or regular follow-up care. Language therapy, orthopedic surgery followed by physical therapy, psychotherapy, medication for hyperactivity, and other services may be provided outside your school so that, in essence, you share responsibility for a case with others. Consider some of the many kinds of professionals who can become involved in the care of special needs children:

Social workers usually gather background information in an intake interview and help organize a case study for other professionals. They may coordinate a case, help a family make medical appointments, or seek out other community resources. In some instances, they work with parents who need to talk about their own personal difficulties or the impact of caring for special needs children.

Psychologists usually administer individual tests to determine the level of intellectual functioning or overall development. They do not have medical training and do not prescribe medication. They may also give treatment or psychotherapy for emotional or interpersonal problems in children and their parents.

Psychiatrists are medical doctors who have additional experience with interpersonal problems. They can prescribe medication and can conduct interviews to determine "mental status," emotional functioning, and difficulties with interpersonal relationships. They carry out treatment or therapy for these same problems.

Neurologists are medical doctors particularly concerned with how the brain and the central nervous system influence behavior and development. They may refer children for electroencephalograms (EEGs) and other special medical procedures. Subsequently, they may prescribe medication for seizure disorders or hyperactivity.

Pediatricians are medical doctors who assess normal child development and treat medical diseases that occur in children. They are often assisted in their private practice or in a neighborhood health center by a *nurse practitioner,* a nurse who has received special training to care for more routine problems under the supervision of a physician.

Nurses often work on a team and perform a variety of functions, such as family counseling or setting up a treatment program in the home to work on feeding, toileting, or sleeping routines.

Physical therapists are concerned with the motor coordination of bones and muscles. They evaluate motor functioning, perform or design exercises and activities to strengthen muscles, and prevent or correct deformities.

Occupational therapists also carry out developmental assessments, paying more attention to fine motor and perceptual functioning. They may design programs to help children develop skills in such everyday tasks as self-feeding or dressing.

Speech and language therapists evaluate a child's sound production, technical difficulties in producing words, or use of oral communication. They design programs or exercises to improve articulation and voice tone or to isolate problems in word fluency, grammar, or syntax. Occasionally they may refer children to an *audiologist,* a specialist who is able to test a child's hearing.

Behaviorists do not belong to a specific professional grouping but may be found among any of the specialists listed above. They use behavior modification or reinforcement techniques based on operant conditioning principles.

When specialists share responsibility with you and the family for a child's treatment plan, there is an added responsibility for all the adults involved. Unilateral decisions are no longer feasible. If you want to change a child's program or schedule or if you want to work on particular problem issues with parents, you must first check out your ideas with the other professionals involved. Unless you coordinate carefully, you may unwittingly plunge a family and yourself into conflict between two opposing sets of advice. For example, you may advise a family that their child should spend another year in your class to consolidate her gains; yet an outside language therapist may simultaneously encourage a family to apply to a specialized school that deals with language problems. Or you may be philosophically opposed to the use of medication to control hyperactivity, yet a child in your class is under the care of a neurologist who has prescribed a drug. In yet another example, a deaf child may respond well to sign and gesture language in your class, but his speech therapist does not believe in any visual means of supplementing oral speech training. Each of these dilemmas represents an active controversy in a field of expertise other than yours. Your job is to keep in close touch with other professionals to try to understand better how all of you are helping.

For some families, the different kinds of help they receive may seem conflicting. Not infrequently, they have ambivalent feelings about the use of certain types of treatment for their child. While it may be appropriate for you to raise questions, it is not usually helpful to a child or family if you impose your doubts or personal opinion on the situation or take sides. If confusion in the family persists or honest differences in treatment continue, a joint meeting of members from each agency involved is critical. You may have to take the initiative to call people together. Often you will discover that differences were largely semantic, due to lack of information or distortions in the parents' understanding. Whenever possible, take the opportunity to accompany a special needs child and family to various medical evaluations or therapeutic follow-ups. Your observation of a speech or physical therapist at work with a child or your joint conversation with a parent and neurologist may be more helpful than a dozen phone conversations or written reports.

When a new special needs child is first assigned to you, review his history of evaluations and treatment. Telephone the doctors or therapists currently involved in his or her care to introduce yourself, invite them to visit, and determine what kind of future conferences or communications will be needed. If you lay such groundwork at the beginning, you will save time later, and your work with the child will be more challenging and rewarding.

More about You and Us

Whether in supervisory or consultative relationships or in the classroom, teachers differ in the way they learn. They give priority to different elements in their work with children. We are aware of two distinct styles of learning about children, which we call "intuitive" and "cerebral." As you read this section, think about your own style and the styles of the persons with whom you work.

Teachers with an "intuitive" style get acquainted with child and family by immersing themselves deeply in the details of their student's life. From this process they evolve an empathic understanding of how he or she thinks and feels. They arrive at a formulation of a child's difficulty by using their own selves, feelings, and experiences as major resources. Interventions are seldom framed to place primary emphasis on age norms, skills, or performance.

By contrast, teachers with a "cerebral" style have clearer expectations for children at particular ages. They are less likely to adjust to a child by understanding how he might feel; instead, they learn to change their expectations or find better ways to convey those expectations to him. They make adaptations in their approach by observing a child's behavior and relying heavily on their knowledge of developmental milestones or other frameworks of thought.

Whichever type of helping adult you are, you have warm feelings for children. You simply go about solving the problems at hand in different ways. You will probably use supervision and consultation in different ways, too. If you are an "intuitive" person, you value learning to think through a problem and to apply a theoretical framework, and you relate your learning to what you feel. You welcome questions from supervisors or consultants if they help to make more explicit what you have observed or felt. "Self" is your guidebook. On the other hand, if you are a "cerebral" person, you learn by hearing how someone else might think through a problem and relate it to a theoretical structure. You tend to conceptualize problems and observations and measure children's developmental profiles against common age expectations.

No one neatly fits these categories. But the recognition that adults learn and operate differently and give or receive help according to different styles is essential to working with people. To fully appreciate individual differences among children and adults takes time—perhaps a lifetime. When each of us is valued for his or her uniqueness and individuality, "special needs" will need to be redefined. Learning and behavior problems will only exist as challenges to our understanding of what makes us human beings.

Bibliography

Abramovitz, A. B. *Group Consultation with Teachers.* Second Wisconsin Institute on School Administration and Mental Health. Madison, Wis.: Wisconsin State Board of Health, 1963.

Berlin, I. N. "Teacher's Self-Expectations: How Realistic Are They?" *School Review,* Summer 1958, pp. 134–43.

Braun, Samuel J. "A Guide to Early Childhood Education for Mental Health Personnel." *Psychiatric Opinion* 11, no. 5 (October 1974): 29–34.

Caplan, Gerald. *Concepts of Mental Health and Consultation and Their Application in Public Health Social Work.* Children's Bureau Publication no. 373–1959. Washington, D.C.: U.S. Government Printing Office, 1959.

———. *Principles of Preventive Psychiatry.* New York: Basic Books, 1964.

Farley, Gordon K. "Mental Health Consultation with a Head Start Center." *Journal of Child Psychiatry* 10, no. 3 (July 1971): 555–71

Frank, Thomas, and Gordetsky, Sharon. "Child-Focused Mental Health Consultation in Settings for Young Children." *Young Children* 31, no. 5 (July 1976): 339–44.

Furman, Robert A. "Experiences in Nursery School Consultations." *Young Children* 22, no. 2 (November 1966): 84–95.

Glidewell, John C. "The Professional Practitioner and His Community." *Mental Health Section Newsletter of the American Public Health Association,* January 1969.

Guerney, Bernard G., Jr. *Psycho-Therapeutic Agents: New Roles for Nonprofessionals, Parents, and Teachers.* New York: Holt, Rinehart and Winston, 1969.

Hollister, William G., and Husband, Grant W. "Inservice Mental Health Education Through Group Experience Workshops." *American Journal of Public Health* 42, no. 9 (September 1952): 1071–77.

Jersild, Arthur T. *When Teachers Face Themselves.* New York: Columbia University Press, 1955.

Kiester, Dorothy J. *Consultation in Day Care.* Chapel Hill, N.C.: Institute of Government, 1969.

Murphy, Lois B. "The Consultant in a Day-Care Center for Deprived Children." *Children* 15, no. 3 (May-June 1968): 97–102.

Newman, Ruth G. *Psychological Consultation in the Schools*. New York: Basic Books, 1967.

Rosen, Jacqueline L. "The Remembered Childhood Self as Forecaster of Teacher-Child Relations." ERIC Microfiche ED 083 224, 1972.

Sarason, Seymour B.; Davidson, K. S.; and Blatt, Burton. *The Preparation of Teachers: An Unstudied Problem in Education*. New York: John Wiley and Sons, 1962.

Stein, Myron; Beyer, Evelyn; and Ronald, Doris. "Beyond Benevolence—The Mental Health Role of the Preschool Teacher." *Young Children* 30, no. 5 (July 1975): 373–76.

Tanruther, Edgar M. *Clinical Experiences in Teaching for the Student Teacher or Intern*. New York: Dodd, Mead, 1968.

Appendix

Children's Books Addressing Difficult Life Issues

Before reading a book that deals with a sensitive issue to children, you should be thoroughly acquainted with the book. In some cases the pictures may be relevant, but the text is too lengthy. Improvise by using the pictures to tell a simpler story. Some aspects of a story may emotionally overburden some children, so you must use judgment and tailor the text to each child's individual needs. When there is no book written about the specific issue a child is concerned about, writing your own book about the child and his concerns is often very helpful. Young children appreciate the simple effort of a few sheets of paper stapled together with primitive pencil drawings and text elaborating their concerns.

The books listed below are suggested for children between the ages of three and six:

Death

Aliki. *Go Tell Aunt Rhody*. New York: Macmillan, 1974.
This old folk song deals with the death of the "old grey goose" as an

---

This annotated bibliography was prepared by Sally Kear Braun.

ordinary event in everyday life. The bright colors and strong drawings contribute greatly to this book's appeal to young children.

Brown, Margaret Wise. *The Dead Bird*. Reading, Mass.: Addison-Wesley, 1958.
Children find a dead bird and bury it. The text and illustrations are appropriate for three year olds as well as older children.

DePaola, Thomas A. *Nana Upstairs and Nana Downstairs*. New York: G. P. Putnam's Sons, 1973.
A little boy shares his concerns with his mother about his grandmother's death.

Fassler, Joan. *My Grandpa Died Today*. Illus. Stewart Kranz. New York: Behavioral Publications, 1971.
When David's grandfather dies, David struggles to understand and accept his death.

Gackenbach, Dick. *Do You Love Me?* New York: Seabury Press, 1975.
Walter accidentally kills a hummingbird. This book gently describes Walter's feelings and tells how his parents help him deal with this reality.

Grollman, Earl A. *Talking About Death: A Dialogue between Parent and Child*. Boston: Beacon Hill Press, 1970.
This is required reading for parents and teachers. The author helps adult and child to cope with helplessness, guilt, loneliness, and fear.

Harris, Audrey. *Why Did He Die?* Illus. Susan Dache. Minneapolis: Lerner Publications, 1965.
A mother answers her young son's questions about death in a simple, rhyming poem.

Miles, Miska. *Annie and the Old One*. Boston: Little, Brown, 1971.
This Indian legend deals well with the themes of old age and death.

Stein, Sara Bonnett. *About Dying: An Open Family Book for Parents and Children Together*. New York: Walker, 1974.
Loss of a pet and loss of a grandparent are the issues dealt with in this book. Anger, confusion, mourning, fantasy, and death are discussed in ways helpful to both child and adult.

Tresselt, Alvin. *The Dead Tree*. Illus. Charles Robinson. New York: Parents' Magazine Press, 1972.
The life cycle—growth and decay—of a huge oak tree is told in accurate fact and rich artistic detail.

Viorst, Judith. *The Tenth Best Thing about Barney*. Illus. Erik Blegvad. New York: Atheneum Publishers, 1971.
The death and burial of Barney the cat are told in a sensitive, yet matter-of-fact way.

Warburg, Sandol S. *Growing Time*. Illus. Leonard Weisgard. Boston: Houghton Mifflin, 1969.
The story of a young boy who grieves when his dog dies of old age. Although

written for an older child, it can be read to a four or five year old who has had this kind of experience.

Zolotow, Charlotte. *My Grandson Lew*. Illus. William P. DuBois. New York: Harper and Row, 1975.
Six-year-old Lew wakes at night and tells his mother he misses his grandpa, who died when he was two. He and his mother reminisce, finding consolation together.

Divorce

Adams, Florence. *Mushy Eggs*. Illus. Marilyn Hirsh. New York: G. P. Putnam's Sons, 1973.
In this story, the vigor as well as the struggles of living in a single-parent home are portrayed. Feelings of sadness and anger are expressed when a favorite baby-sitter leaves.

Berger, Terry. *A Friend Can Help*. Milwaukee, Wis.: Advanced Learning Concepts, 1974.
A girl tells her friend how she feels about her parents' divorce.

Goff, Beth. *Where Is Daddy?* Boston: Beacon Press, 1969.
A sad story for preschoolers tells about a small girl whose parents separate.

Grollman, Earl A. *Explaining Divorce to Children*. Boston: Beacon Press, 1969.
The author deals sensitively with divorce, helping the adult as well as the child come to terms with his feelings.

Kindred, Wendy. *Lucky Wilma*. New York: Dial Press, 1973.
A young girl and her father adjust to their new relationship in which they spend only Saturdays together.

Lexau, Joan M. *Emily and the Klunky Baby and The Next Door Dog*. New York: Dial Press, 1972.
Emily's divorced mother has so many responsibilities that she doesn't have much time for Emily.

———. *Me Day*. New York: Dial Press, 1972.
Rafer worries that his divorced father will forget his birthday.

Rogers, Helen S. *Morris and His Brave Lion*. Illus. Glo Coalson. New York: McGraw-Hill, 1975.
This is a sophisticated story about Morris and his divorced father. When his father finds it too painful to visit his son, Morris reaches out to him.

Sanek, Muriel. *I Won't Go Without Father*. Chicago: Albert Whitman, 1972.
Steve is afraid to go to open house at his school without his father. When his uncle, grandfather, and neighbor accompany him and his mother, Steve is much happier.

Stewart, Robert. *The Daddy Book*. Illus. Don Madden. New York: American Heritage Press, 1972.

Using amusing illustrations, a variety of roles for fathers is depicted. Although divorce is not mentioned, the scenes lend themselves to encouraging discussion among the children about experiences with fathers.

Zindel, Paul. *I Love My Mother*. New York: Harper and Row, 1975.
Illustrated in a vivid manner much like pop art, this book tells of a young boy's world with his mother and without his father.

Handicaps

Fassler, Joan. *Howie Helps Himself*. Illus. Joe Lasker. Chicago: Albert Whitman, 1975.
Beautiful artwork and a simple, honest text reveal the struggles and successes of a young child physically handicapped with cerebral palsy.

Klein, Gerda. *The Blue Rose*. Photos Norma Holt. New York: Lawrence Hill, 1974.
The story of how Jimmy, a retarded child, is different and yet loved.

Lasker, Joe. *He's My Brother*. Chicago: Albert Whitman, 1974.
A young boy tells about his brother who has learning problems. With beautiful illustrations and affectionate detail, the negative and positive aspects of the reality are explored.

Levine, Edna. *Lisa and Her Soundless World*. Illus. Gloria Kamen. New York: Behavioral Publications, 1974.
This story tells of a child living in a soundless world, using lipreading and hearing aids.

Nadas, Betsy P. *Danny's Song*. Pittsburgh: Family Communications, 1975.
Though Danny can do many things, he sometimes cannot keep up with his brother and sister. The hurt and anger Danny feels wearing crutches and braces is well-portrayed within the context of a loving, supportive family.

Stein, Sarah Bonnett. *About Handicaps: An Open Family Book for Parents and Children Together*. New York: Walker, 1974.
As the title suggests, this series brings difficult issues into the open. In this book, people's negative reaction to those with handicaps is discussed with constructive suggestions for parents and children confronted with this situation.

Wolf, Bernard. *Don't Feel Sorry for Paul*. Philadelphia: J. B. Lippincott, 1974.
Paul was born with incompletely formed hands and feet. Text and beautiful photographs show Paul's action-filled life over a two-week period during which he learns to ride a horse.

Illness and Hospitalization

Galbraith, Kathryn O. *Spots Are Special*. Illus. Diane Dawson. New York: Atheneum Publishers, 1976.
Playful illustrations portray Sandy's bout with chicken pox. She overcomes the boredom of isolation from her peers by using her vigorous imagination.

Rockwell, Harlow. *My Dentist.* Illus. Harlow Rockwell. New York: Greenwillow Books, 1975.
Illustrations are unusually strong, clear, and informative. The dentist seems to be sensitive to children's needs.

———. *My Doctor.* New York: Macmillan, 1973.
Two qualities make this book about doctors and hospitals outstanding: the artwork is unusually uncluttered and attractive and the doctor is a woman.

Rey, Margaret and Rey, H. A. *Curious George Goes to the Hospital.* New York: Scholastic Book Services, 1966.
This lively monkey's antics in the hospital intrigue, entertain, and educate children.

Segal, Lore. *Tell Me a Mitzi.* Illus. Harriet Pincus. New York: Farrar, Straus and Giroux, 1970.
In one of the three stories, Mitzi is the first to get sick, but soon the whole family is in bed with a cold. Grandmother arrives in time to take care of everyone. The illustrations and the story are appealingly and affectionately homey.

Sharmat, Marjorie W. *I Want Mama.* Illus. Emily McCully. New York: Harper and Row, 1974.
A young girl's predicament of wanting her "mama," who is hospitalized, is well expressed and illustrated.

Stein, Sara Bonnett. *A Hospital Story: An Open Family Book for Parents and Children Together.* New York: Walker, 1974.
The feelings of a young child are explored both before and after a tonsillectomy. The author stresses the importance of preparing the child to enter the hospital. Parental presence at the hospital is encouraged.

Weber, Alfons. *Elizabeth Gets Well.* Illus. Jacqueline Bloss. New York: Thomas Y. Crowell, 1969.
Attractive full-page watercolor drawings accompany the story of Elizabeth's appendectomy written by a Swiss child psychiatrist. The information, imparted in warm and factual detail by the drawings and text, is helpful for any child anticipating a hospital stay.

Wolde, Gunilla. *Tommy Goes to the Doctor.* Boston: Houghton Mifflin, 1972.
Not only does Tommy get a shot from the doctor, but he becomes a pretend doctor himself and gives his teddy bear a shot, too. Bright pictures and text make this attractive to three and four year olds.

Birth of a Sibling

Alexander, Martha. *Nobody Asked Me If I Wanted A Baby Sister.* New York: Dial Press, 1971.
A little boy expresses his feelings about the birth of his sister.

Byers, Betsy. *Go and Hush the Baby.* New York: Viking Press, 1973.
An older sibling is able to quiet and entertain the new baby in his family. The book stresses positive family relationships.

Flack, Marjorie. *Angus and the Cat*. Garden City, N. Y. Doubleday, 1971.
Angus the dog is jealous when his family gets a new cat. After displaying a bit of hostility toward the cat, Angus finally capitulates.

———. *The New Pet*. Garden City, N. Y.: Doubleday, 1943.
The author does not romanticize a child's feelings toward a new baby. Gradually and reasonably, the new baby is regarded with affection by his two siblings.

Gerson, Mary Jean. *Omoteji's Baby Brother*. Illus. Elizabeth Moon. New York: Henry Z. Walck, 1974.
The story, set in Africa, deals with a new baby. Written in rich language, careful attention is paid to the details of everyday life in Africa.

Greenfield, Eloise. *She Come Bringing Me That Little Baby Girl*. Illus. John Steptoe. Philadelphia: J. B. Lippincott, 1974.
When everyone pays attention to the new baby, Kevin feels rejected. With help from his mother, he discovers compensations in his role as big brother.

Keats, Ezra Jack. *Peter's Chair*. New York: Harper and Row, 1967.
Peter's feelings toward the birth of his sister are illustrated by his difficulty in giving the new baby his outgrown chair. When he is certain of his parents' love, Peter is able to share.

Krasilovsky, Phyllis. *The Very Little Boy*. Illus. Ninon. Garden City, N. Y.: Doubleday, 1962.
Young children appreciate this story depicting the signs of growth of a little boy. First, he grows old enough to use a sled and work at the workbench. Finally, he is old enough to push the carriage for his very little sister.

———. *The Very Little Girl*. Illus. Ninon. Garden City, N. Y.: Doubleday, 1953.
The story is the same as the preceding Krasilovsky work, but a little girl is the main character.

Scott, A. H. *On Mother's Lap*. New York: McGraw-Hill, 1972.
The best part about "mother's lap" is that she has room for both her son and the new baby.

Stein, Sara Bonnett. *That New Baby: An Open Family Book for Parents and Children Together*. New York: Walker, 1974.
This book tells about the anxieties and fears children have when their mother goes to a hospital to have a baby. The author makes helpful suggestions to aid a family with a new baby.

Lost and Found

Brown, Margaret Wise. *The Golden Egg Book*. Illus. Leonard Weisgard. New York: Simon and Schuster, 1947.
A little rabbit thought that he was all alone in the world until the egg sitting next to him hatches a friend—a baby chick. Beautiful illustrations and the drama of the tale never fail to capture the attention of three and four year olds.

———. *The Runaway Bunny*. New York: Harper and Row, 1942.
Children delight in hearing this tale of a little bunny who tests his mother's love by running away. Mother rabbit demonstrates the strength of the bond by always finding her ingeniously hidden baby rabbit.

Eastman, P. D. *Are You My Mother?* New York: Random House, 1960.
Baby bird hatches when his mother is away from the nest. Children identify with his humorous search and reunion with his mother.

Freeman, Don. *Corduroy*. New York: Viking Press, 1970.
Corduroy was a lonely little teddy bear living in a department store until he is bought and loved by Lucy.

Kellogg, Steven. *The Mystery of the Missing Red Mitten*. New York: Dial Press, 1974.
A simple story, appealingly illustrated, of a little girl and her puppy who have set out to find her lost red mitten.

MacDonald, Golden. *Little Lost Lamb*. Garden City, N. Y.: Doubleday, 1945.
After a series of adventures, a little boy and his dog find the lost lamb before nighttime.

Mayers, Patrick. *Lost Bear, Found Bear*. Illus. Beatrice Darwin. Chicago: Albert Whitman, 1975.
The lost and found theme is meaningfully resurrected for a three year old by simple text and clear, easily understood drawings.

Ormondroyd, Edward. *Lost and Found Theodore*. Illus. John M. Larrecq. Berkeley: Parnassus Press, 1966.
Lucy really loved her bear, Theodore, who was "comfortable and smudgy," but she was sometimes careless. This is a convincing tale of loss and reunion.

Tresselt, Alvin. *The Mitten*. New York: Lothrop, Lee and Shepard, 1964.
This is a Ukranian folktale in which a child loses his mitten in a forest and animals reclaim it. The book is charmingly illustrated and humorously written.

Van Stockum, Hilda. *Little Old Bear*. New York: Viking Press, 1962.
There is an underlying theme of recycling in this tale of a teddy bear rescued from a garbage can. Though he is old, he is loved more than the new teddy.

Welber, Robert. *Goodbye, Hello*. Illus. Cyndy Szskeres. New York: Random House, 1974.
Irresistible drawings of animals tell this story, which reassures a young child that partings are both ends and beginnings.

Moving

Hoff, Syd. *Irving and Me*. New York: Dell, 1972.
In humorous, cartoonlike drawings, the author tells about experiences of moving that children identify with.

Hickman, Martha W. *I'm Moving*. Illus. Leigh Grant. Nashville, Tenn.: Abingdon Press, 1975.

Clear pictures and excellent text will help a young child with the stress of moving.

Tobias, Tobi. *Moving Day*. Illus. William P. DuBois. New York: Alfred A. Knopf, 1976.
Elegant and clear illustrations are to the point, as is the language in this book. The story is about moving, told from the perspective of a little girl and her teddy bear.

Thompson, Vivian. *Sad Day, Glad Day*. Illus. Lilian Obligado. New York: Holiday House, 1962.
This author is realistic in her portrayal of a child's feelings about moving.

Zolotow, Charlotte. *Janey*. Illus. Ronald Himler. New York: Harper and Row, 1973.
Janey experiences loneliness after her friend moves away.